"This is quite simply one of th[e] [...] Africa. Jean has a remarkable [...] You will feel as though you are [...] the people she has met, and sen...ᵣ ᵤₘₑₜₕᵢₙₔ ₒⱼ ₜₕₑ ₕₑₐᵣₜ ₒⱼ ₒₒₐ for their needs and situations. We enter into their world on their terms, and go away knowing we have been on holy ground."

The Right Rev Harold Millar, Bishop of Down and Dromore

"I loved reading this book. Jean's stories interweave heartache and hope in a way which challenges me about the devastating impact of extreme poverty, inspires me about the response of the global church and enthuses me to become a stronger, more Kingdom-orientated Christian."

Tim Magowan, Northern Ireland Director, Tearfund

"In Journey of Hope we are introduced with sensitivity and realism to the harshness and joy of those who, against 'the slings and arrows of outrageous fortune', remain resolute. When you have read this book you will begin to understand why the grassroots church, often without mission statements or five-year strategies, is not just growing but exploding in this, the Global South. Here you encounter ordinary people who not only believe but who live their lives 'in step with the spirit'."

The Very Rev Dr Trevor W. J. Morrow, Presbyterian Church in Ireland

"Jean Gibson combines her gift of story with her heart of compassion as she bids us listen. What we hear will disturb us. Each person's true story is filled with challenge, struggle and pain far more intense, even brutal, than most of us in the West will ever have to face. But

these are not tales of despair. On the contrary this is a book filled with the faith, hope and love of Christ. We learn afresh from our African sisters and brothers in Christ what it really means to love, follow and trust him."

Rev Donald Ker, Secretary of Conference, Methodist Church in Ireland

"Journey of Hope is a raw account that puts a human face to some of the untold real life stories of sacrifice, courage, hope, resilience, faith, empathy and living the gospel. It is also a portrayal of the co-existence of contrasting cultures brought together by a strong belief in God's faithfulness and social justice."

Margaret Zondo, Program Administrator, International Ministries, Life & Mission Agency, Presbyterian Church in Canada

Also by Jean Gibson

Seasons of Womanhood is a contemporary collection of inspiring stories from women who have faced the reality of life and proved the sufficiency of God's power in many different situations. It covers various stages of a woman's life, from early days through to the final years. Jean Gibson shows us that none of us is alone in our experience and that no situation is beyond hope.

Joyful in Hope tells the stories of eight inspirational women who are facing life with courage and faith, sometimes doubting, but desperately holding on to God and trusting even when they do not understand what is happening. These women reassure us that God reaches out to us in our struggles and that he can bring us through.

JOURNEY OF HOPE

Stories of courage and faith from Africa

Jean Gibson

MONARCH
B O O K S

Oxford, UK & Grand Rapids, Michigan, USA

Published by Monarch Books
an imprint of
Lion Hudson plc
Wilkinson House, Jordan Hill Road, Oxford OX2 8DR, England
Tel: +44 (0)1865 302750 Fax: +44 (0)1865 302757
Email: monarch@lionhudson.com
www.lionhudson.com

ISBN 978 0 85721 295 5 (print)
ISBN 978 0 85721 337 2 (Kindle)
ISBN 978 085721 338 9 (epub)

To those we met on the journey,
who continue to inspire us

Contents

Foreword

I have only just finished reading *Journey of Hope* and, fittingly enough, I am in Africa. I know nobody who has travelled to this mesmorizing continent and seen some of the things that Jean Gibson talks about who has not been changed for ever. This remarkable book will allow you to take that journey.

It would be good for each of us to take some time to walk the dusty roads that *Journey of Hope* takes us along. But be careful: you will have to dodge the goats, chickens, and bicycles stacked with huge bags of grain or tobacco. And keep your eyes open not just for danger but for beauty: "hornbills perched in trees, yellow bustard swooping overhead…tiny dik-dik with their large dark eyes, danc[ing] like dainty ballerinas."

Welcome to Africa – and to the lives of Africa.

You are invited to the wedding of Maria and Mr Mponda. You have already listened in as Maria was introduced to her prospective husband's relatives a few days ago. They had each taken it in turn to give her the traditional advice offered to new brides. The topics were varied: how to look after her new husband, how to organize the household budget, personal cleanliness and how to live according to the customs of her in-laws. But now the great day has arrived. Join her as she sits on a special mat and watches as the groom's family come forward and lay the dowry money down.

Maria is married.

But this is Africa, and coming down the dusty road towards Maria is the spectre of AIDS and the battle for the life of her child.

I think you will enjoy meeting Marcus. Jean Gibson will take you into his house: "about three and a half metres long and three metres wide, a middle wall divides the sleeping area from the living room." You will sit on the upturned beehives that serve as stools – your knees almost touching. For a few moments there will be the traditional Malawian silence and then Marcus will speak: "Welcome to my home…"

And so will begin the incredible story of one young man's fight for education. You will listen as he declares the hope of so many in Africa: "Only education will set us free from the cycle of poverty that has held us."

But if you are looking for an easy read – a satisfying travelogue to while away a lazy Sunday afternoon – perhaps it would be best to take the book back to the shop while you can still find the receipt. Because in many ways this is a disturbing book – some scenes will not only move you, but haunt your memory.

Consider for a moment a little of Nabiki's story. It is her wedding day. Just four weeks ago she underwent "the cut" – the removal of all her external genitalia, a procedure known as Female Genital Mutilation. Normally girls undergoing this would be given a year to recover before being married, but Nabiki's family are poor and, to survive, they need the dowry they will receive for her. Soon the women will come to shave her head in preparation for the

Maasai wedding. Once the celebrations are over she will live in her new husband's village, far away from her home and family. The man she is to marry is sixty years old and already has five wives.

Nabiki is twelve.

She starts to run – as fast as she can – through the bush. Soon the villagers will chase after her, but she manages to make it to the mission. Mary comes towards her, arms outstretched to hug the sobbing child. Nabiki can hardly get the words out: "I don't want to get married today…"

Yes, I was disturbed reading *Journey of Hope*. But perhaps in truth the real danger in life is not being disturbed, not gasping at the unending struggle of lives that are being lived within a nine-hour flight of our homes. The stories that Jean brings to us are, without exception, accounts of faith, courage and determination against what so often seems to be impossible odds.

Back from her travels and safe in her warm home, Jean ends her book like this: "Small inconveniences fade into insignificance in the face of the tragedies we have witnessed." As I turned the last page I felt the same. And yet my main memory of the book is not of tragedies, but of laughter, endurance and… hope.

In spite of all you are about to see and hear, I think you will enjoy this journey.

Rob Parsons OBE
Founder of Care for the Family

Acknowledgments

As in my previous books, I am indebted to all those who have allowed their story to be told. It was a privilege for us to meet each of you and to see how you face each day with resilience and hope. Thank you also to the mission personnel who introduced us to the central characters in this story and expended considerable time and effort to facilitate the writing of the book.

Friends who read parts of the manuscript and offered suggestions were an invaluable help, especially Carolyn Gowdy who has once again been a support and mentor. My thanks also go to Tony Collins and the team at Lion Hudson for all their help and encouragement, and to John Kelly for his help with the photographs.

I could not have carried out the journey in the first place without the co-operation and driving skills of my husband Brian, who sacrificed his annual leave to ensure I travelled safely. The highlight of his trip was being greeted by a young Kenyan who knew of his work in Theological Education by Extension: "We thought Gibson would be very old and fat." Our shared experience of this journey will remain with us for a long time to come.

Introduction

In June 2011, my husband Brian and I set out on a trip through Malawi and Kenya. Having worked in theological education in Kenya for eight years while our children were younger, we were interested to return to Africa and in particular to meet local people who had faced specific challenges in their lives. What we discovered was one person after another confronted by difficult and sometimes tragic circumstances, unbowed by their situation, strong in faith, and determined with God's help to create a better future for their family and community.

In this book, the story of our journey runs alongside the life journeys of those we met on our travels. For both them and us, hope emerges as the theme, as together we look beyond present circumstances to see God working out his plan through his people.

As you read, I pray that you may also experience this hope.

All the stories in the book are true, although in a few instances names and details have been changed to protect identities.

Map of
AFRICA

Kenya

Malawi

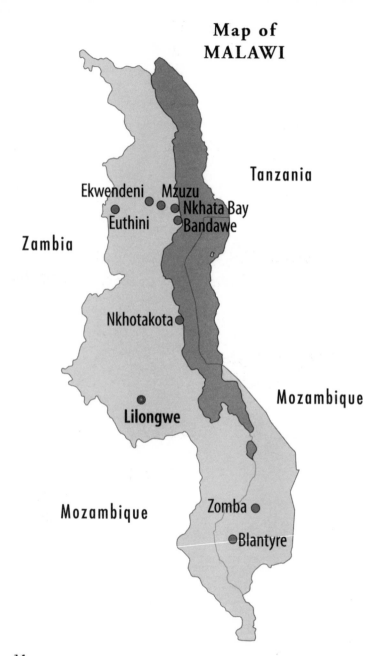

Map of
MALAWI

Tanzania

Ekwendeni Mzuzu
Nkhata Bay
Euthini Bandawe

Zambia

Nkhotakota

Mozambique

Lilongwe

Mozambique

Zomba
Blantyre

Map of
KENYA

1
Joy

The raucous sound cut through my sleep with the persistence of a pneumatic drill. Reaching through the mosquito net for the reading light, I squinted at my watch: 4.00 a.m. After the previous day's journey I had expected to be unconscious until morning, but I hadn't counted on the local rooster. I covered my ears with the blanket and closed my eyes again.

We had arrived in Ekwendeni in the north of Malawi the previous evening, twenty-eight hours after leaving home. Despite having worked in Kenya in the 1980s and having made a number of return visits since, I had had reservations about the journey.

"'Leave Lilongwe Airport; turn left down a small unmarked road shortly after the police checkpoint. When you meet the Mzuzu road, turn left and keep going for 350 kilometres. Don't forget to take the right fork at Mzimba where you see all the signs.'" I read the email aloud to my long-suffering husband in the safety of Ireland.

"What happens if we turn left down the *wrong* small unmarked road?" I worried. "350 kilometres is a long way to go in the wrong direction!"

Pragmatic is his middle name. "We can't get lost in Malawi. There's only one main road going north from the airport."

"That was when you were there years ago," I persisted. "Things will have changed."

In the event, Paul, who delivered our hire car to the airport, wanted a lift to the Mzuzu turn-off, so at least we knew we were heading in the right direction. From my brief research before the trip, I had a vague mental picture of this long, narrow country, surrounded by Mozambique to the south and east, Tanzania to the north and Zambia to the west.[1] The scrubland stretching away on either side of the road was greener than I expected, thanks to the recent rainy season. Small groups of mud-brick houses provided intermittent signs of habitation. The straight, tarmacked road stretched into the distance, devoid of the potholes I was used to in Kenya; for the first part of the journey we met few other cars and were grateful for prior advice to stop in the town of Kasungu to fill up with fuel and use the facilities. The next filling station we saw was in Mzuzu, some four hours later.

Along the roadside Malawian young people, flashing white smiles, proffered a variety of produce as we passed. We were tempted by mangoes and pawpaw, the tastes of Africa, but, conscious of the need to reach our destination before dark, we kept going. Children held out sticks that looked like some kind of kebab. Taking a closer look, I realized they held a row of mice – I could see the tails. We decided to pass on those too.

The landscape became more dramatic further north,

and the road more demanding of Brian's driving skills as we climbed steep hills, dropping down the other side into sharp bends. Light was fading as we approached the city of Mzuzu. Suddenly the road was filled with people making their way home on foot before dark, calling to each other, laughing and shaking hands. Women walked tall and straight, their possessions on their heads: bags of fruit and vegetables, containers of water.

Without warning, a bicycle veered across the road in front of us, bumping across the rough terrain towards some unseen destination. Bicycles wound their way through the crowd on the road, with not just one but sometimes two passengers perched behind the cyclist; I stared in disbelief as a sizeable lady balanced side-saddle on the back of a bicycle, a large bundle on her lap. It was not until the next day that I realized bicycle taxis were equipped with a cushioned seat behind the saddle for the use of passengers.

In Mzuzu we turned left towards Ekwendeni. The sun was setting behind the hills, its beauty distracting us from the vibrant display of life on the road ahead. At the police checkpoint we showed our documents and were waved through when we explained we were going to the mission. Half an hour later our headlights picked out the sign for Ekwendeni Hospital, and we wound our way up the dirt road past the huge church, the hospital buildings, and the school for the visually impaired, through staff accommodation to the home of our friends. We clambered from the car, stiff from the journey but delighted to see a light in the doorway and a familiar face.

"Welcome to Ekwendeni! You made good time."

"Yes, we were determined to get here before dark. It's so good to see you."

"Come on in. Is this all your luggage?" Robin grabbed our case and guided us into the house.

Robin and Helen had worked in Malawi for many years, Robin in theological education and Helen in the women's empowerment programme. They welcomed us with Irish hospitality, understanding our exhaustion after the journey and generously providing our two basic needs – food and bed.

Under the mosquito net, with the light out, I was almost asleep when I became aware of a scratching noise. I was instantly awake.

I had lived in Africa for eight years without a mouse doing me any harm; I turned over and tried to relax. But I had failed to tuck the mosquito net in round the mattress, leaving the ends lying loosely on the floor. If the mouse was under the bed it could run up the inside of the net while I was sleeping. I dragged myself out from under the net, carefully slid my feet into shoes, and tucked the net firmly under the mattress. A quick check around the room with the reading light revealed nothing untoward. Brian was snoring peacefully. I crawled back under the net, tucked in the final section, and settled myself for sleep. The scratching resumed but this time I felt secure. Suddenly a heavy thump started my heart racing again. Whatever was sharing our bedroom was much more than a mouse. Convincing myself that nothing could get through my tightly tucked-in net, I closed my eyes.

In the morning, a few hours after the rooster, we rise to the joy of African sunshine. Outside our bedroom window, I discover an extensive rabbit hutch on stilts, built by a local carpenter whom Helen is encouraging in various projects. The source of the scratching and thumping from the night before becomes clear. Helen is introducing the local populace to the potential of breeding rabbits as a business and an addition to their diet. They are bound to taste better than mice.

In the kitchen, Mr Shonga has started work and is delighted to have someone to talk to. He tells me about his family as he finishes washing the dishes.

"In the Ngoni tribe we used to marry many wives. Things have changed, and these days we don't have so many. I just have two."

"Why do you need more than one?" I wonder in my naivety.

"The problem is that some wives are lazy," he says seriously. "Sometimes they refuse to work, some are too talkative, some are too quick to leave the family if they are not happy, so in that case it is better to find another. Men are very few and women are many. A woman needs a man to avoid poverty. She needs him to help her, so that is why she gets married, even if he already has other wives. Some of them misbehave and torture their husbands, if the men have been drinking, by not allowing them to sleep in the house with them, or by refusing to make them food."

Mr Shonga turns from the sink to set out the vegetables he is preparing for the evening meal. His mind is still on the complexities of couple relationships.

"The man has to be fed, so man and wife need to sit down and discuss together if there is a problem, rather than quarrelling. Many times it is not that we want more wives, but because of how the women act. If a wife moves away from her husband she can only be the second wife of someone else. No young man can marry her again as his first wife."

Bemused by this introduction to local family life, I wander out of the back door of the house, my eye drawn to the panorama of hills on the skyline. No one had told us northern Malawi was so beautiful. The thatched-roof shelter a few yards from the house, another creation of the local carpenter, offers protection from the sun and invites me to relax for a while. With care, I try out one of the irregular chairs and take time to absorb the view. The tall leaves of the banana plants rustle like frayed paper in the early June breeze; alongside them the stocky papaya trees with their heavy green fruit stand impervious. A gecko negotiates one of the supports of my shelter, and I remember the time my parents came to visit us in Kenya years ago when our children were small. Faced with my mother's horror at a gecko running up the wall in her bedroom, three-year-old Sarah Jane reassured her, "Don't worry, Granny. They're our friends; they eat the mosquitoes." Birds call constantly in the trees around, the rabbits scamper through their elaborate hutch, and I might be tempted to doze off in the sunshine if it wasn't for that rooster still crowing in the distance. Does it never sleep?

Later, Helen's friend Joy Mzinza joins us for a meal. Enjoying chicken casserole and rice, we get to know each other as we share our different experiences. The meal ends and Joy and I sit on, talking together.

"In 1979 I was studying in Lilongwe Teacher Training College. When I came home to Chitipa for the holidays, I met Jarvis Gondwe, a young livestock officer with the Agriculture Development Marketing Corporation (ADMARC), who had come to visit a teacher friend in the town. We struck up a friendship and three years later, when I had finished my teaching course, we got married."

Joy's features grow animated as she recalls the wedding in Mzimba, Gondwe's home area. After a church ceremony in the village of Engalaweni, the wedding party and guests travelled to Gondwe's village, four kilometres away. There the celebrations continued late into the evening, with singing, dancing, presenting gifts of money to the young couple, and enjoying the traditional wedding meal of chicken, rice, and *nsima*,[2] washed down with alcohol-free sweet beer.

"In the towns, people sometimes had a wedding cake, but it was not part of our village wedding. Our celebration was quite traditional," says Joy with a wry smile.

A few days later they left Mzimba to travel to Blantyre, in the south of Malawi, where Gondwe was working and where Joy managed to get a teaching post. The following year their first daughter was born, followed by two more daughters at two-yearly intervals. Gondwe spent a year at college in Kenya, studying bee-keeping, and the resulting honey business augmented their income. Their comfortable life was suddenly disrupted, however, by the news of

Gondwe's posting to Karonga, hundreds of kilometres north, up near the Tanzanian border. With their three small daughters, the family left the home where they had lived so happily and started again in Karonga.

Six months later, on 15 May 1989, Joy was at home with her children when her parents and other relatives all arrived together to see her. Quite apart from the distance they had travelled, she realized from their faces that it was not a casual visit.

"We have just heard from ADMARC," her father said. "They have asked us to come and see you – Gondwe has had an accident."

Joy knew it was serious. "What happened?"

They struggled to tell the story. That morning, Gondwe had been on his way to Mzuzu for a meeting when his vehicle left the road and crashed into a tree, crushing the door on his side of the car and breaking his ribs. With the accident site many kilometres from the nearest hospital and his injuries complicated by internal bleeding, Gondwe died just as he reached Rumphi Hospital. Others in the vehicle were injured but Gondwe was the only one who died. Joy could not take it in.

"I was very shocked to hear he was already in the mortuary. If someone has been sick it is different, but if someone has left home in the morning feeling well – just to be told he is dead and in the mortuary, that is a great shock. I was young. I had had no experience of death before that. I didn't know what to do."

Together Joy and her family travelled to Gondwe's home village, where the young couple had been married so happily seven years before. Two days after the accident, he was buried there in his home place. People travelled long distances to come to the funeral, relatives and friends of the young couple and of the wider family. Joy existed through it all, stunned, trying to take in what had happened.

After the funeral service Gondwe's friend Revd Mvula came to speak to her, concerned about her future.

"Where would you like to live with your children?"

"I would like to go to Ekwendeni." It was an automatic response.

"Why Ekwendeni?"

"It's associated with the people who fear God and I think I will be supported by those people, rather than staying far from a church. I'd like to live there."

His response was kind. "I will try to talk to people to see if there might be a teaching job for you in Ekwendeni."

It was at the time of the funeral that Joy realized she was pregnant again – another baby to care for, and Gondwe did not even know about it.

Together with her children, and accompanied by Gondwe's mother and brother, Joy travelled back to the home in Karonga that they had so recently set up together. The following day, her brother-in-law asked for all the keys of the house and went through each room, making an inventory of the contents. All that Joy owned had suddenly become the property of her husband's family. Although the house was owned by ADMARC, the company told Joy she could continue to have the use of it for up to three months, and that they would help her relocate when she felt ready to do so.

One month after the funeral, Joy was invited back to Gondwe's village for a special ceremony. His family prepared sweet beer, while Gondwe's male relatives sat down under a tree, in a semi-circle from oldest to youngest. Then Joy was asked to kneel before each of them in turn and offer them a drink from the calabash of sweet beer given to her by the women. Conscious of all eyes upon her, Joy complied with this request, ending with the youngest male of the family. The first part of the ceremony completed, the women took her into the house and handed her some clothes; with a start, she realized she was holding a pair of trousers and a shirt and tie that had belonged to Gondwe.

"Take these and give them to the one you have chosen to be your husband," was the demand.

Too late, Joy understood that the offering of the drink had been her opportunity to approach each man and select one to marry. She was horrified at the thought.

"No, I will not do it," she protested.

Traumatized by the whole procedure, grieving for the husband she had loved and lost so recently, she was unable to control her emotions. Through her tears, she tried to articulate her thoughts.

"First, in normal circumstances, it is not the wife who chooses a husband but the husband who chooses the wife. How can you ask me to choose? Secondly, those men already have their own wives – I am a Christian, and it is not allowed in my church to become a second wife."

Undeterred, they insisted, "You are young; you cannot remain without a husband."

Joy refused to comply. "When God was taking my

husband, he saw how young I was. He is the one who will take care of me."

Eventually her pleas prevailed and one relative intervened.

"Leave her alone. If she has refused, she will have to stay alone."

It was agreed. The matter ended and Joy was allowed to return to her home.

Looking back, she understands the family's position. "It was natural. Because my husband's family paid a dowry for me, I belonged to them." But, several years later, she is glad she was determined to stand against the pressure of her culture.

"Those men, the relatives of my husband who said I should marry them, have now died of AIDS and left their wives and children behind, so, if I had married one of them, I would have the same disease." She believes that God guided her then and gave her the strength to stand firm in what she believed to be right.

At the end of the school term, once she had harvested her maize and removed it from the cob, Joy informed ADMARC that she was ready to move to Ekwendeni. Packing up her home, she set out on the journey, conscious that she was leaving many memories of happier times but with the reassurance that she was going to a place where she would find the support she needed to pick up her life again and care for her young family. Gondwe's mother and brother accompanied her on the journey.

With the family wedged into the vehicle together with all Joy's possessions, they reached Ekwendeni in the middle of the night and spent the remaining hours of darkness in the vehicle, trying to sleep. In the morning, Joy went to meet the headmaster of the primary school where she would be working. He was glad to see her but explained that her house would not be available for another three days, when the present occupant was due to leave. In the meantime she could use the needlework room. Joy began to organize the offloading of her luggage but her brother-in-law was already sorting it out, informing her that she could keep only the kitchen utensils. Everything else was going to his home. In despair, Joy watched him repack her furniture, including her bed – almost everything she owned, so many items that held memories of her life with Gondwe.

She says, "They took virtually everything, including the curtains, even the mattress for us to sleep on. It was not easy. And the children were young: they were six, four, and two years old." At the last minute her brother-in-law relented and allowed her to keep her sewing machine. Then, as the little family stood and watched, the in-laws left with all Joy's possessions, continuing their journey to their home in Mzimba in the ADMARC vehicle. That night, and for many nights to come, Joy, uncomfortable because of her advancing pregnancy, slept with her children on the floor.

Three days later, as promised, she moved into her new house, which she was renting from the Women's Guild. She now had two rooms, a bedroom and a sitting room, although only the bedroom had a window. The kitchen and toilet were outside. It was small but it was her own, and she was free from the oppressive presence of her in-laws.

She settled in and gradually made the little space into

a home for herself and the girls. As she had foretold, the members of the Women's Guild and the wives of the local church ministers came to comfort her and support her in her new life as a widow.

She remembers, "They taught me the word of God, and that I should take Jesus as my husband and concentrate on taking care of my children."

Gondwe's relatives continued to appear from time to time, collecting other items from her house. Joy's father was philosophical: "Give them everything they demand. God is going to provide all you need."

Acting on his advice, Joy treated them with kindness when they came, offering them food, somewhere to sleep, and money for transport back to their home.

"I decided to treat them well and not take revenge. My husband was a good man. It was not his wish to die and leave me behind. It was not his fault things turned out like this."

Sometimes her children would look at photographs of the house the family had lived in before their father died and remember how things used to be. Their young minds could not understand.

"All these things that were in our house – where are they now?"

"They are in your father's home place with his family. We cannot get them now."

A few months later Joy's baby was born, a boy at last after three girls. Grieving that Gondwe would not see him, Joy treasured this little life that symbolized their love and would have brought him so much joy.

Once she was settled in Ekwendeni and her position became known, men began to appear from time to time to propose marriage. Joy turned them down, always remembering a conversation between herself and Gondwe before a hypothetical situation had become a reality.

"If I die, what will you do?" he used to say.

"I will not marry; I will remain with my children." Joy knew that children would usually have to be left with a relative rather than be taken to a new marriage. "What about you, if I die myself?"

"I will stay for one year, and then I will look for a wife to do the cooking and to care for the children," was the practical Gondwe's reply.

Joy told the men she had made a vow to her husband not to marry, and she had to keep her promise.

Two years later, in 1992, she was offered a teaching post in Ekwendeni Girls High School. The change of job allowed her to move house, with more space for her growing family. She was able to buy two mattresses, one for herself to share with her youngest child and one for the three girls. Gradually she acquired simple items of furniture for the house and new curtains for the windows, and was grateful to God for his answers to her prayers and his provision for her family.

As the children grew, the school fees needed for the four years of secondary school became a problem. She managed to find fees for the first three years for Temwa, her eldest daughter, but, as the other girls started secondary education and also needed fees, it became more difficult. Ruth, an Irish teaching colleague, kindly offered to pay Form 4 fees for Temwa. On finishing school, Temwa's desire to go to nursing college came to the attention of Shirley, a nursing tutor at Ekwendeni Hospital, who undertook to sponsor her through college. Joy was touched and delighted by her generosity.

"I only had to provide soap and a few things; Shirley looked after her uniform and everything else, and helped her until she finished college." Temwa now works as a nurse in Karonga District Hospital and is married with a daughter of her own.

In 2001, Joy became ill. High blood pressure and heart failure kept her at home for a complete school year on medication, unable to teach. Friends and well-wishers rallied round, praying, sharing the word of God, giving her hope that she would recover. When she became depressed at the length of her illness, they would take her out and help raise her spirits. Her friend Ruth taught her how to use cross-stitch embroidery to make cards, something she could do without too much exertion. Ruth provided her with the materials and thread, which were unobtainable in Malawi, and sold the cards in Ireland, providing Joy with a small income while she was unable to teach. Joy was overwhelmed by all the support she received from the Christian family.

The following year, although still very weak, she returned to work. She was grateful to be well enough to work, but in 2005 she was posted to a secondary school in Euthini, a remote area far from her friends in Ekwendeni. She missed their companionship and support.

However, her work enabled her to pay secondary-school fees for her second and third daughters, Julia and

Gomezgani. When Julia finished school, she wanted to go to college to study computing.

"I don't have enough money for college fees," protested Joy.

"Can you look for money?" Julia insisted. "The course is starting in January and I really want to go to college to study."

Joy was keen to encourage her daughter's interest in education but knew the college fees were beyond her meagre income. Returning to Ekwendeni, she discussed the matter with her friends Helen and Robin. She thought that if she could borrow money to buy material, she could make school uniforms for Ekwendeni Girls School and supplement her teacher's salary.

Robin's response was measured. "We don't have much money in the house today. Why don't you come back tomorrow and we'll think about it in the meantime?" That night Joy slept at a friend's house and returned the next day to resume the discussion. She was met by a smiling Robin.

"As soon as you left yesterday, we had an email from home telling us that the Girls' Brigade have raised some money and set up a fund towards the education of girls in Malawi. Julia can be the first to be sponsored from this fund."

"Praise God for that." Joy was overcome by the timing of this dramatic answer to her prayers.

"Tell Julia to come so we can take her photograph and send it to Ireland. It will be good for the Girls' Brigade to see the people they are sponsoring."

Once procedures were in place, the system worked

well, and in the end both Julia and Gomezgani successfully completed a computing course at Mzuzu University under this scheme.

Her son, who had always had a special place in Joy's heart because of the circumstances of his birth, sadly also brought her great heartache. In 2009, she discovered that he was about to become a teenage father, and as a result both he and his girlfriend were being expelled from school. She was heartbroken. It was not what she wanted for her son. At the same time, in the midst of her sorrow, Joy wanted to react in a Christlike way.

Taking the girl into her home, she cared for her until the baby was born. Then, willing to pay for them to finish their education, she encouraged both young parents to go back to school. Her son now attends class during the day while his wife is at home with the baby, who has grown into a lively toddler. Later, the mother attends evening classes while Joy and her son share the babysitting. Joy is glad to see her son beginning to shoulder responsibility for his wife and child, although once again her salary is stretched to the limit.

"Now I look after everybody – the father, the wife, the son. When it happened at first, I really cried because I was so upset. But the girl is also an orphan, with no father or mother. She was living with a stepsister from another mother. You can imagine the problems that causes. I think now, as well as being a mother, she has found a mother herself. That's why I am sending her back to school. If she is educated she will be able to care for her son. I am just showing them all the love of Christ because we don't know the plan of God and what he has in store for us all in the future."

Today, widows in Malawi are still at the mercy of their husband's family, even though they are officially protected by law. Joy says, "The husband's family are not allowed to take everything from her but it still happens. If the wife dies, they will take the wife's sister and give her to the husband so that the sister can look after the children, but some women still mistreat their sister's children. One man I know was given his wife's niece when his wife died, so that she could care for the children. After two years the man died of AIDS, leaving the young girl with a new baby. Soon the baby died from AIDS, and then the young mother also got sick with the same disease." In the midst of these situations, Christian women in Malawi encourage each other to live out the life of Christ.

Joy's dream is to return to live in Ekwendeni, to start a tailoring business there and eventually to build her own house. She is realistic about the timing, however.

"Each time I want to start a project there is another thing that is hindering me. But when God shows his plan, then I can do it. My husband's family cannot help me, or my relatives, only God. He has done it before. I am trusting in him. I will wait for God's time."

2

Marcus

"*Yimani!* Stop!" Mrs Chihana, Helen's colleague in the women's empowerment programme, waves us down as we drive out of Ekwendeni. With a cheery greeting, she passes a bundle through the window of the Land Rover and wishes us well for our journey. The smell that wafts through the vehicle indicates freshly made *mandazi*, the delicious fried breads similar to doughnuts that are eaten as a warm snack all over East Africa and are especially popular as breakfast food. It is 6.00 a.m., so she has been busy early this morning. I settle back in my seat, touched by her kindness. I understand why they call Malawi "the warm heart of Africa".

We are on our way to Euthini, a remote area about three hours' drive west from Ekwendeni, towards the Zambian border. Not far from Ekwendeni, we leave the tarmac and the Land Rover comes into its own as Robin negotiates the ruts and bumps of the dirt road. As the vehicle shudders its way over the uneven ground, I remember what it means to travel in Africa. Every bone in my body rattles and I wonder if my vertebrae will all be in the same place by the time we get there.

Golodi, a young man from Ekwendeni, has joined us for part of the journey, catching a lift to his home village, where he lives with his uncles. Although the Land Rover is a long wheel base model, I assume the vehicle has its full complement of passengers with the five of us on board, plus some rabbits in the back which we are taking to Marcus Harawa, the young man we will visit in Euthini. Not far along the road, however, a man flags us down, requesting a lift to a funeral. When Robin invites him into the back of the Land Rover, three women appear at a run and climb into the vehicle with a flurry of baskets and laughter. As I watch in disbelief, they hold open the door and more pile in, squeezing into spaces that seem impossible. They shove the rabbits and other baggage unceremoniously out of the way and we make a desperate attempt to save the *mandazi*. By the time the door is firmly shut, I count seven smiling faces bobbing around in the back. A chubby baby gazes unperturbed from the sea of colourful *chitenges*[1] that the women wear wrapped around them as skirts. Helen and I are wearing them ourselves today.

"Thank you, thank you." They speak Chitumbuka, but their joyful demeanour indicates their gratitude for the lift. As we meet no other vehicle on the road, I wonder how they would have got to the funeral with all their foodstuffs if we had not passed by. Presumably they would have walked. They laugh and chatter happily in their confined space and eventually indicate where they want to get out, about sixteen kilometres along the road. With many handshakes, smiles, and waves of farewell, they tumble out of the vehicle and make their noisy way down a path out of sight.

The next stop is to drop Golodi at his village, which entails leaving the "main" road we are on and bumping over a narrower track through the scrubland. We leave him at a small village of houses built with the traditional mud bricks and thatched roofs. We will collect him again on our return journey.

Back on the road, we drive through fields where the tobacco crop has been harvested, past barns where the leaves are hung and cured. Malawi is the world's most tobacco-dependent economy, but falling prices due to the world economic crisis and the international anti-smoking lobby have led to reduced production. Farmers are being encouraged to focus instead on crops such as coffee, cotton, and sugar.

Given the condition of the road and the various stops along the way, the journey to Euthini takes longer than planned, but eventually we reach the buzzing trading centre. The excitement of the market entices us to unfold our legs from their cramped positions and interact with the cheerful populace promoting their produce on the busy main street. Silver piles of *usipa*, small dried fish, line the sandy roadside; brightly coloured plastic bowls and cups vie for space with more traditional baskets; school uniforms hang primly from a cord stretched between two poles. An amazing array of flip-flops extends along the street like some bizarre multi-coloured keyboard for feet. This is the place to come for all one's household needs and for all the local gossip.

Marcus Harawa arrives to meet us, shakes hands, greets us politely in English, and welcomes us to his area. At one of the stalls we buy fresh rolls to take with us for lunch. The other prerequisite is an assortment of "sodas", the ubiquitous fizzy drinks found in the remotest parts of Africa. Our selection ranges from Coca-Cola and Fanta Exotic to local varieties Coco-Pina and Cherry Plum. Equipped with our purchases, we pile back into the Land Rover and prepare to follow a narrow track across the barren landscape.

As we leave the trading centre, it is obvious that ox cart is the preferred mode of transport, which makes perfect sense, given the terrain. A group of them stand bunched together, waiting for business. Nearby, a small mud building with a tin roof incongruously advertises "Connect and recharge here". Inexpensive and efficient, the mobile phone has permeated Africa as successfully as Coca-Cola.

We bump our way across the open countryside, the track having almost disappeared. Eventually abandoning the Land Rover, we continue for a short distance on foot, until we come upon a small collection of mud-brick houses where Marcus lives with his family. The ground between the houses is swept clean and I get the impression that Marcus has gone to some trouble to have the place looking its best for our visit, from the outdoor cooking area near the houses to the tidy pit latrine further away. An assorted group of adults and children jostle through the doorway of the larger house; someone tries to explain but I cannot remember what all the relationships are.

Marcus shows us his own recently completed house, he and his brother having made and fired the bricks themselves from local anthill clay. About three and a half metres long by three metres wide inside, a middle wall divides the sleeping area from the living room. Someone has donated oblong beehives, which Marcus has upended and used as seats around three of the walls. There is just room for the four of us to sit down with him, our knees almost touching. We wait for a few moments in the traditional Malawian silence before he welcomes us officially to his home. With the pleasantries completed, the others retreat to the shade of a tree while Marcus and I talk about his life.

"When I was only three years old, my parents separated, leaving my mother to take care of us on her own. My father offered no further assistance to his wife or children. I was the second of four children and the eldest boy." Marcus looks down at his hands as he goes back to his earliest memories.

As he grew, Marcus kept asking questions about his father. Even as a young child, he realized it was difficult for his mother to manage on her own.

"Where is my father? Why does he not live with us?"

"Marcus, I have only primary-school education. Your father wanted a more educated wife. That is the main reason he left us."

As a child, Marcus pondered the significance of education and the effect that the lack of it could have on every aspect of life.

Left alone, the natural place for Marcus's mother to go was to her own mother in Ekwendeni. Her mother's house was already full, as her brothers, the children's uncles, were still living at home and were largely unsympathetic to this sister returning with her four children. Marcus's mother took care of her little family as best she could, doing "piecework", a variety of odd jobs, in the hope of being given something in return. She gathered and sold firewood, she sold sweet potatoes and cassava. At one stage she was employed by a relative to sell ice fizzes in the market – frozen juice in little plastic bags.

When Marcus was ten years old, his mother decided to move from Ekwendeni to another township. Although it meant finding rent for a house, life was more peaceful for the four children and their mother once they had left all their other relatives behind. The children moved to the local primary school and their mother continued to sell fruit and vegetables to earn money for their daily survival and basic needs.

One day Marcus's aunt, his mother's sister, offered to take Marcus's older sister to live with her and her husband. They would offer her a home and, in return, she could help out in the house. For Marcus's mother, it was an opportunity to ease the burden of caring for so many. His sister was in Standard 8 by this stage, her final year at primary school.

Not long after she had moved to her aunt's home, however, the thirteen-year-old became pregnant, abused by her aunt's husband. In despair, Marcus's mother brought her daughter back home again. With the new baby, there were now five to care for. The younger siblings did not really understand what was happening and just accepted this new playmate who had come to join them. There were no repercussions.

"Because the incident happened within the family, nothing was done," says Marcus, shrugging his shoulders. "My aunt stayed with her husband. She was upset, but she could do nothing. The story just died. That baby girl is now twelve years old."

The following year, an older uncle, who was a head teacher in a primary school and had a farm about 100 kilometres from Ekwendeni, telephoned Marcus's mother one day with another suggested solution for her problems. If she and the children would come and cultivate his tobacco crop as tenants on his farm, he would give her a share of the profits after the first year and she could start cultivating her own crop.

Encouraged by the possibilities opened up by this idea, his mother agreed. The family moved to live on the farm and the children transferred to the primary school where their uncle was head teacher. Marcus, now a twelve-year-old in Standard 6, worked on the farm with his brother and sisters, as agreed. There was nothing unusual about this; Malawi has the highest occurrence of child labour in southern Africa, with the vast majority of five- to fourteen-year-olds involved in agriculture. An estimated 78,000 children work on tobacco estates.

Unaware of the risks of poisoning due to the absorption of nicotine from the surface of wet tobacco plants, Marcus and his siblings worked, often for long hours, without protective clothing. For children, the symptoms of nicotine poisoning – severe headaches, abdominal pain, muscle weakness, coughing, and breathlessness – are more pronounced than in adults. Child labourers can absorb up to fifty-four milligrams of dissolved nicotine, which is comparable to smoking fifty cigarettes a day.[2]

With the tobacco harvest over, however, the promised money was not forthcoming. When questioned, the uncle claimed he had made a loss, not a profit, so there was no money for the family. He was willing to give them food in exchange for their work, but nothing else. Disappointed and discouraged, the family were left with the status of slaves, working for their uncle in order to survive. They could see no way out of the situation.

Almost two years later, Marcus completed his Standard 8 examinations and had the opportunity to go to a community secondary school. Still working for his uncle, he approached him as the obvious first source of the required school fees. He was met with an unequivocal refusal.

"No, I have no money for school fees."

"Then what can I do? I have completed Standard 8." Marcus was desperate.

"The only thing you can do is repeat Standard 8."

Marcus and his mother agreed that this was not an option. For the first two weeks of term he attended Form 1 of the secondary school, but, without fees, he was not allowed to continue. The following term he began again, attending for the permitted first two weeks of term, but once again he was told he would have to leave. For six weeks he remained at home, working for his uncle so that the family would have food, but determined somehow to find the necessary fees for school.

Then some friends from school arrived at his house with amazing news.

"If you have 300 kwacha you can come back to school at Chaboli. The headmaster has announced it."

Surprised but delighted, Marcus and his mother

managed to gather together the money and he set off for school, eager to begin again.

"Look, I have come with my money this time." He presented his kwacha to the headmaster.

"What do you mean?" the headmaster was confused. "Three hundred kwacha is the sum those pupils have to pay who want to sit the General Certificate of Education examination. Your friends have got the information mixed up. I wasn't talking about school fees, but about exam fees."

Marcus could not believe what he was hearing. Although it had seemed too good to be true, he had been convinced by his friends. He had glimpsed the possibility of attending secondary school, had felt it within his grasp. He could not abandon hope now. On the spot, he made a decision. He was not going back home again; he would find the fees somewhere. Writing a note for his mother, explaining that he had gone to Ekwendeni to look for school fees, he handed it to a friend and asked him to deliver it.

At 7.00 the next morning, he set off on foot towards Ekwendeni. Used to walking long distances, he kept going until 4.00 p.m. Unsure of the way, however, and afraid of getting lost, he stopped to ask a villager for help.

Looking at the tired fourteen-year-old, the man said, "Look, it's getting late. Why don't you go to the chief's house tonight and ask for accommodation?"

Relieved by this idea, Marcus followed the man's suggestion and approached the chief, saying, "I am on my way to Ekwendeni to get school fees and need somewhere to sleep."

Perhaps impressed by the determination in the young man's face as much as by his story, the chief took him in and gave him food and a bed for the night.

Early the next morning, as soon as it was light, Marcus set off once more, determined to reach Ekwendeni that day. Towards the end of the morning, however, he realized he was getting very tired and that his legs had begun to swell. He knew he had the 300 kwacha still in his pocket, but was reluctant to use it for transport, wanting to keep it towards his fees. If he could raise 700 kwacha altogether, he would have enough for one term. Overcome with tiredness, he lay down and slept beside the road on the dry, sun-warmed earth. Some time later he woke, feeling more rested but realizing that the day was passing quickly and he still had a long way to go. As he stood, he saw a lorry approaching, and flagged it down in the hope of getting a lift. When he explained his situation, the lorry driver agreed to take him to Ekwendeni in exchange for thirty kwacha. Given the state of his legs and the time of day, Marcus reckoned it was worth it, so he paid the thirty kwacha and reached Ekwendeni that evening.

He went straight to his grandmother's house, hoping that she would at least give him food and shelter. What he did not expect, however, was that she did not recognize the fourteen-year-old on her doorstep as the same boy who had left with his family four years earlier. When he explained who he was, her whole expression changed and she burst into tears.

"How have you come all this way alone?" She asked as she ushered him into the house.

"I walked most of it and then I got a lift in a lorry for the last part. I had to come and look for school fees because my uncle will not help and my mother has no money."

As Marcus talked through the problem with his grandmother that evening, it was a relief to be able to share it with someone who understood the situation. She soon came up with a suggestion.

"Why don't you go and see your father? He is working, so he should have money. Perhaps he will help you with your fees."

The next day, acting on this advice, Marcus found his father, who agreed to give him fees for the first term. His grandmother matched it by giving him fees for the second term, and one of his uncles provided money for transport back home. By this time his mother, distraught at the thought of Marcus walking that distance all alone and worried about what might happen to him on the way, had followed him to Ekwendeni. Reunited, they returned home together, relieved that the story had ended as well as it had.

Marcus managed to gather money together for the third term's fees, but, as he thought about the year ahead, he realized he had to change his strategy. He was always going to struggle for fees in the remote area where they were living. He begged his mother to allow him to transfer to school in Ekwendeni, where there would be more opportunity for him to find someone to help with his fees and to get piecework in the holidays. Reluctant to see him go, but realizing it was his best chance of obtaining secondary education, his mother agreed. His grandmother provided a home for him in Ekwendeni and he took every opportunity to work when he wasn't at school, constantly saving up money for fees. At the end of the second year he did well in his examinations. The following year saw the same pattern. He had found a formula that seemed to work for him.

At the end of Form 4, however, his examination results were disappointing. Expending so much energy on gathering fees together and living so far from his family were beginning to take their toll. He worried about his mother, still working on the farm with his brother and sisters. He needed to repeat the year if he wanted to do well enough to go to college. He began to explain to people that he was looking for fees once more, and one day shared his feelings with his friend Katoa. Moved by the young man's desperation, Katoa's mother made a suggestion.

"Why don't you go and see Mrs Quinn? She is an Irish lady who sometimes helps people with school fees."

The following morning, Marcus followed up this suggestion and found that there was indeed a fund which could be accessed for help.

"It was such a relief to me when I explained the problem to Mrs Quinn, because she and her husband were interested in me as a person. They even encouraged me to go and see my mother in the holidays. They came to visit our home and, when they saw the situation, they helped us with everything. They said, 'From this time on we are going to help you. You don't need to worry about searching for fees.' It was like a load taken from my shoulders. That year I took my exams again and had much better results."

Marcus sat the university entrance exam but failed to

get a place. He was very disappointed.

"I could not remain doing nothing because of all our problems. I knew it was only education that would set us free from the cycle of poverty that held us. When the Quinns found out I had not got into university, they suggested applying to the National Resources College, which offers courses in practical subjects such as irrigation, agriculture, horticulture, and nutrition. I decided to take their advice and, when I was accepted for the course, they helped to provide everything I needed as a student. During the holidays I came to see them, and they continued to give me advice and help me in so many ways."

In April 2009 Marcus's grandmother died. He returned to Ekwendeni for the funeral, sad to lose this significant figure in his life. The Quinns were away on leave and he missed the stabilizing comfort of their presence. A few months later, he suffered an even greater blow when his mother also passed away.

"That was a challenge to me, as my mother was both mum and dad to us. Wherever she was, we felt that was our home, especially since our dad abandoned us and our uncles turned against us; we had only her. When she passed away I didn't know what to do. I could only say, 'God knows. He has good plans for us.'"

With their mother's death, the young people had to leave the house they had shared with her. Marcus was in his second year at college, his younger brother and sister were still employed as tenants of their uncle, and his other sister had gone to work for a different uncle some distance away. Marcus felt lost; the family had split up and he had no base to come home to. The Quinns had become the closest thing to parents that he had. When he came back to Ekwendeni in the college holidays, he talked to them about the family's situation.

"Why don't you look for another place to live, where you can all be together?" they suggested. "That would free you from being bound to your uncles."

It was a daunting task for a twenty-three-year-old, but, on consideration, Marcus decided it was the only way to keep the family together. Shouldering his responsibility as the eldest boy, he went to the village headman in the area of Euthini where the family was well known, and explained his situation. The sympathetic headman agreed to let him have a plot of land of about 200 m^2 where the family could be together again. He encouraged Marcus to come in the holidays and prepare the land for cultivating. He even donated some fertilizer to get him started.

There were already some dilapidated houses on the land, left by a previous owner, but the ground was dry and dusty. It was going to take a great deal of work to grow anything. Marcus managed to fix up a dwelling and very soon the family were ready to move in. It was a novelty to have a place of their own, free from their uncle's control, and by the time Marcus graduated from college they were well settled. As head of the family, he accepted responsibility for the others as the natural order.

"I am responsible for the whole family," he explains. "They treat me as the parent, even though I am twenty-four. I am heading the family. My older sister got married and has three children plus the one from before, so now she has four. Her husband left her and went to Johannesburg, so I said, 'Sister, don't worry. Just come and we will be helping one another.' So now we are eight. That is why I have built a separate house for myself."

Once Marcus had successfully obtained his Diploma in Agriculture in 2010, the Quinns sat down to discuss the next step with him.

"What is your plan now, Marcus? You are trained in agriculture and you need to use it. We want to empower you to become independent so that you don't need to keep coming to us for help. What do you want to do?"

Marcus was clear. "I want to rear chickens at home. If I buy young chickens, I can rear them and have eggs to sell."

"Very well. We'll help start you off. What do you need?"

Marcus decided the first step was to build a house for the 100 chickens he hoped to rear. Keen to show me how his ideas are beginning to take shape, he walks with me to inspect the new chicken house, built with local mud bricks. Almost complete, it is an impressive structure, many times the size of his own house. He is eager to get it finished and have the chickens in place. The logistics of transporting the birds to such a remote location do not deter him, nor does the challenge of getting his eggs to the buyers. He is hoping to get a contract with the nearest secondary school, about twenty kilometres away, so that he has a steady market.

Many other ideas are burning in his mind. "I am just waiting for the chickens now. I want to organize farmers in this area so they can get different types of chickens, some for meat and some for eggs. I have two groups of farmers who are keeping chickens. I want to use my training to help others. We are also making fertilizer and growing trees." He shows us a neatly laid-out plot where he has already started planting seedlings. Pigs and goats are next on his agenda.

"I thank God for bringing us Mr and Mrs Quinn. I call them my parents. Psalm 146 says, 'The Lord sustains the fatherless and the widow.' Don't worry if you are an orphan; God will be there. I have found this to be true. He has provided the Quinns for us. You have seen today how it is not easy to reach here by vehicle, but they still come to visit us. I pray for them every day. We are here because of them; otherwise we would be scattered everywhere."

Marcus is active in his local church, chairing the youth work, organizing youth events, involved in fundraising and preaching on Sundays, helping with many aspects of church life. I ask him how his faith developed.

"At first I was just going to church as normal but when I met the Quinns it was a turning point for me. I said, 'Why is this happening to me? How is it that there is someone who is protecting me and caring for me?' I realized I needed to turn to Jesus as my personal saviour. He is doing good things for me and I need to be loyal to him. I really mean it. What I saw in the Quinns' life was a good testimony; you can see everything of God in them. They assist us spiritually; they talk to me about God. They gave me a Bible so I started to read it because if I want to please God I need to know what he says. Mr Quinn gave me books and a commentary to study, so it helps in preaching. I don't know how to thank them but I know it is only God who can thank them on my behalf."

We sit outside on more beehives, a thatched roof shading us from the sun as we share our bread rolls and sodas. Once we have made extensive farewells to the family, Marcus escorts us back to our vehicle and we set off on the return journey. Deeply touched by all that I have heard and seen, I have a renewed awareness of the powerful effect of Christlike living on the lives and hearts of others. It is a theme that will recur frequently during our travels.

We retrace our way to Golodi's village and stop to greet his extended family, including his very elderly grandfather. We pile back into the Land Rover, accompanied by an indignant chicken, a gift from the family. A short distance down the road, we are flagged down by the same cheerful group of women we helped in the morning, now on their way home from the funeral. They climb aboard, delighted to see us, greet us as old friends, and settle themselves happily beside the chicken. The sad event has obviously not depressed their spirits.

Later that evening, a few of us go to the Pine Tree restaurant outside Mzuzu. Thrown together as a group of people far from our own country, we enjoy the novelty of a meal out under the stars. As we talk and relax after the long day, my mind keeps flitting back to the small mud house in Euthini, where a young man is eating with his family and trusting God to bring him through all the challenges that lie ahead.

3
Mphatso

"I am the mother of ten children by nine different fathers." Mphatso pauses for effect then bursts out laughing. "I love to shock people. They don't know how to respond when I say that. But it's true. These children bring such joy to my life."

At nine o'clock in the morning, Mphatso is taking a break to meet me. As Director of the Livingstonia Synod AIDS Programme (LISAP), her day begins early, but she welcomes me with Malawian hospitality into her office in the extensive LISAP complex in Ekwendeni. Rearranging her tailored jacket and smoothing out her smart skirt, she grins across at me, exuding an air of mischief as we begin to talk. But life was not always such fun. Her expression becomes more serious as we settle into our chairs.

"I was very young when my parents divorced, so I never knew them. My mother married again and had to leave me with my grandmother; she is the first person I can remember."

I remark on the number of stories I have already heard about divorce in my short time in the country. Mphatso nods.

"It is very common, especially in the villages, for people to get divorced and remarried. People get married early, before they know what marriage is all about, and they don't have time to get to know one another. Young girls tend to get married while they are still in their teens, when they're not really mature. Then when they realize they are not happy, it's easy to get divorced. The best way of counteracting early marriage is education. If people do not continue in school, they get married; what else is there to do? We need to encourage our young people to stay in school and pursue their education before they think of marriage. Of course, the problem is families cannot afford the school fees, so poverty encourages early marriage."

Reverting to her own life story, Mphatso fills me in on her disturbed early years. She lived with her grandmother until she was the right age for school, when her aunt Beatrice in the south of the country offered to take her. Her primary-school years were spent moving between various relatives, depending on who could afford to send her to school.

Every house she went to had different ways of doing things. When she was in Standard 8 her aunt had a baby and Mphatso had to come out of school to look after the baby for two months. Her friends joked, "When they call out your name for the class register we say, 'She has a baby.'"

She comments, "It was difficult because, wherever you are living, you accept life as it is. I realize now there were times when the situation was not ideal for me as a child. But because I really wanted to go to school, I was willing to put up with anything. If someone sent me to school, that was all I asked."

When she finished primary school and was selected for secondary, her aunt could not afford the fees. Fortunately at this point her uncle Khoti stepped in, undertaking to see her through her four years of secondary education.

When she was in Form 3, however, Khoti went to the UK for further studies, assuring Mphatso that the money for her fees had been put in place. Soon after his departure, his wife, Lire, began to complain that money was short. She set up a business, requiring Mphatso to make *mandazi* through the night until 2.00 a.m. so that she could sell them in the offices in the morning. People seemed to like them and business was brisk. Then one day someone said to her, "We want to buy from you because your aunt told us this money is for your school fees." Young as she was, Mphatso realized there was something not quite right about the situation.

As the following term began, money was short once more. One day Lire ran out of patience.

"I don't have any money because I am using it all for your school fees," she burst out. "Why does your mother not contribute to your fees? The mother who bore you should be the one taking care of you."

As Lire continued her tirade, a deep resentment began to grow in Mphatso's heart. "Why did my mother do this? Why didn't she go to school herself instead of getting married? From what I am listening to now, it would be better if I was not here at all, if I had never been born."

Desperate to escape from all the complaints, she decided to go to Blantyre, where her aunt Beatrice and her uncle Chinyengo were living, but of course she had no money for the bus fare. Persistent, however, Mphatso kept asking for the money until, pushed to the limit one day, Lire took her to the bus and bought her a ticket for Blantyre. Mphatso was delighted. As soon as she arrived, she went straight to her aunt Beatrice and explained the need for school fees. Beatrice was shocked.

"But your uncle Khoti said he had arranged to pay your school fees. I have no money for fees."

"Then I will give up school," said Mphatso, frustrated by all the problems with fees.

Aunt Beatrice was taken aback. "Let's go to your uncle Chinyengo and see if he can help."

Her uncle, though sympathetic, was also short of money.

"No, I can't manage your fees, because your cousin is at school and I have to pay those fees."

"Then I have no option," repeated Mphatso. "I will have to stop going to school."

Everyone was shocked; it was well known in the family how much she loved school and how well she was doing. Chinyengo, genuinely wanting to help, made a suggestion. "Wait for a week so that I can do some piecework and find extra money for fees. But remember your friends will already have started school."

"I don't mind," said Mphatso. "If I can go to school late in the term, it is better than having to miss it altogether."

For a week, Mphatso waited while Chinyengo worked to obtain the necessary money. When he finally produced the fees, she returned to school, overjoyed and triumphant that she was able to do it without any further recourse to

Lire, who had complained so much about the drag on her finances. Mphatso was already nurturing a dream in her heart: she wanted to be a nurse one day. She was determined to do all in her power to make that a reality, no matter what the obstacles might be.

Owing to all the upheaval, Mphatso finished secondary school with lower grades than she expected. On her uncle Khoti's return from the UK, he was surprised at how alarmingly her grades had dropped since his departure. Not realizing all that had gone on in his absence, he offered to pay for her to repeat her final year in a private school, but Mphatso was unwilling to let him pay anything more. Instead, she sent off applications to a number of nursing colleges and was thrilled to be accepted for Nkhoma Nursing School in Lilongwe.

The strict training in this establishment was a challenge on which she thrived, strengthening her determination to be a nurse whatever the demands. Only about one-third of the students who started the course managed to complete the three years, but Mphatso's resolve saw her through and on finishing she was immediately offered a job in the paediatric and maternity wards of Nkhoma Hospital. One year later, sponsored by Memisa, a Dutch organization now known as Cordaid, she went to South Africa to upgrade to a Diploma in Nursing and Midwifery.

South Africa was a culture shock. Mphatso had not realized the extent to which language and culture would cut her off from those around her. She explains, "If you are black in South Africa, people expect you to speak Zulu, or Xhosa, or Sotho, one of the many local languages. When you don't, they just think you are too proud to use the local language. It made life difficult for me there."

At that time, South Africa was going through the transition from apartheid to democratic government, in preparation for the first universal elections in 1994. Although English was the official teaching language, Mphatso found that Afrikaans was often the language used for patients' notes on the wards and sometimes even for teaching, when the teacher forgot that she was in the class. Patients wanted to speak to her in Afrikaans or Zulu. She had no choice but to pick up some of the language.

Some of her colleagues offered to help. "Mphatso, when you answer the phone, this is what to say…" They coached her in a few sentences so that she would not be left speechless on the telephone. It was some time before she understood the reaction she was getting to her carefully practised phrases and realized she had been the butt of a practical joke. The first words she had learned were swear words. When Louise, a close Afrikaans-speaking friend from Malawi, came to visit her in South Africa, she was shocked by her colourful vocabulary. By that stage Mphatso had realized what had happened, but enjoyed feigning innocence to obtain a reaction. She continued to drop the words into conversation, until her colleagues surrendered. "OK, Mphatso, now that's enough. We don't want to hear it any more."

Despite her struggles with the culture, Mphatso emerged as best student at the end of her three years. Back in Malawi, she worked in paediatrics before being appointed to a training post in the nursing school. Just over a year later, further sponsorship from Memisa gave her the opportunity to return to South Africa to train in nursing education, administration, and community health for another three years.

Her second South African course began in 1998. This time her studies were somewhat disrupted when she met and fell in love with a Malawian student who was studying landscape architecture. Mphatso's timetable for her life as a dedicated career woman was turned upside down by this unexpected turn of events. The relationship flourished, and when Mphatso completed her studies in 2001 they parted reluctantly, Mphatso to return to Malawi, leaving Bambo Mulauzi to finish the final year of his course. They had, however, made plans for a wedding in October of the following year, as soon as they could be reunited. In the meantime, Mphatso moved to Ekwendeni to teach in the nursing college there.

In February of that year, Bambo Mulauzi completed his finals, did a live presentation to the panel and was told he had passed the examination. As he left the room, however, he began to feel unwell. He realized he could hardly walk, never mind drive to his sister's house as planned.

He phoned his friend. "Baba, I can't drive. Can you come and pick me up? I'm sitting outside the college."

When Baba arrived, he was dumbfounded. "What has happened? You were doing a presentation a short time ago and now you look like this?"

After carefully helping him into the car, Baba drove him to his sister, Namaseko, who couldn't believe how he looked. When she had last seen him at the weekend he had been fine, able to cook and interact normally with his friends. Next morning she took him to hospital, where he was admitted, but by the time she came back in the evening to visit, he was semi-conscious. The following day he was in kidney failure and his blood pressure had dropped. He was taken into intensive care.

Mphatso's sister, also in South Africa at this time, phoned to alert her to what was happening. At first the sisters reassured each other that it was probably fatigue after working so hard for his finals.

"He is tired," said Mphatso's sister. "He has been working day and night to finish all he needed to do for his course. He just needs to rest for a while."

Very quickly, however, they realized that Bambo Mulauzi's condition was deteriorating. Namaseko phoned Mphatso and told her to come. Mphatso started out immediately, but it was a difficult journey at the best of times, requiring three different buses just to reach Lilongwe. After an overnight stop there she travelled to Blantyre, from where she would take the early bus the following morning for South Africa. Namaseko was now sounding distressed on the telephone.

"Take any bus," she told Mphatso. "It doesn't matter which one, bad or good."

At 5.00 the next morning, just before boarding the bus, Mphatso received a phone call to say that Bambo Mulauzi had died.

Mphatso wipes away a tear as she recalls the trauma of receiving the news.

"He died after only three days in ICU. It was so quick. It was only a week since he had been well and doing his exams. I was devastated. I couldn't believe he had gone."

Mphatso retraced her steps to Lilongwe in a state of shock, at times hardly knowing what she was doing or thinking. It was as if she were watching someone else go through the motions of travel. In Lilongwe she went to her friend Louise, who took her in and cared for her until Bambo Mulauzi's body was brought to Blantyre a week later. Together they travelled to his home place of Ntcheu for the burial.

As they made the journey, Mphatso could not help but think back to a previous relationship she had had while in Nkhoma Nursing College. Although she had been very fond of the young man, she had felt she was too young to marry and wanted to wait. Not understanding her feelings, he broke off the friendship and got married to someone else. It had left her hurt and distrustful of men. During the ten years since that experience, she had steered clear of any close attachment.

"He had been a very close friend to me and up to this day we are still good friends. But I was disappointed in him and I thought, 'If this good friend of mine can do this, then every man will do it.' I waited all these years till I trusted someone again, then he dies just like that. I made a decision after his death – this is the end; I am not going to marry."

Mphatso found it very difficult to come to terms with her loss. Bambo Mulauzi's passing and the thoughts of what might have been tortured her waking hours and haunted her nights. Any funeral she attended caused her to relive his death all over again. Each time, she cried as if it had just happened. Yet through it all she held on to her faith in God.

"I have been a Christian since 1987, so God carried me through all this. I knew that in everything that happens in life, God has a purpose. I knew that, although it hurt, there was somebody greater than myself. God was with me and his love engulfed me. Also friends were so good; they gave me courage to go on."

Although tempted to despair, as she reflected on her life and all that she had come through, Mphatso realized she still had much to be thankful for, including the opportunity to work in a job she found enjoyable and fulfilling.

"I told God I needed to give back to him what he had given me. I was conscious of the plight of many girls who had dropped out of school and got married, not because they wanted to but because of their home circumstances. Many of them were in the situation I was in when my parents divorced. It would have been easy for me to grow up like any other Malawian child, without going to school, without finding a home, being a stranger in my own village. That's when I decided I was going to give back something of what I had received. I couldn't do everything, but I could at least try to help others the way others had helped me.

"Despite all the problems I faced growing up, I could still see love in the eyes of the people who were taking care of me. They had their own children. It would have been very easy for them to say, 'You are not staying in our home; we cannot help you,' but they put up with me and I was still able to go to school. I feel I owe them a great deal. There is no way I can repay what they have done for me, because, for me to be where I am now, it was God working through those people. So I made a decision. Whatever I can do, I will do; whatever I can manage, I will manage."

From that point on, Mphatso started taking in children. Since finishing her first college course at Nkhoma and starting work, she had taken over the payment of school fees for her younger brother and two sisters. While she was in South Africa, however, one sister had died, leaving an eighteen-month-old boy. While still at school, her other sister also had a child, who was now four years old. Her sister and the two children were the first to come and live with her, allowing her sister to continue in school.

More children came who needed care, gradually filling her house. There are now ten she refers to as her own children, for whom she is totally responsible. She pays school fees for others, maybe up to five a year – some distant relatives, some not.

She says, "I am trying to be a true Malawian because in Malawi you never live alone; you always have an extended family. Even people who are married, who have their own children, will always have some extended family with them. The difference with me is that I have never been married or had a child of my own, but it is a joy to me to raise these children. These are my family."

She counts off on her fingers the stages her children have reached. One is now doing a Master's degree in Educational Policy and Leadership in Chancellor College in Zomba. Another is doing an education degree at the same university. Two are working, two are still in primary school, and four are in secondary school.

She jokes about her inability to turn children away, saying with a chuckle, "I tell people I have had tubal ligation now; no more children. Trouble is, I think the tubal ligation doesn't work well, as I seem to get pregnant again!"

While working at the nursing college, she was also teaching prevention of HIV/AIDS in the community. Looking at the different methods used to prevent the spread of HIV, Mphatso was touched as she engaged with the feelings of the women she was trying to help.

"There are different methods of preventing HIV transferring from mother to baby and we teach them all to the mother, but here in Malawi we still tell the mother it is best to breastfeed your child for the first six months. We tell her there is formula, which you can feed your baby, and there is breast milk, which might be infected. Yet because of the possible side effects of formula milk – through lack of water, inability to accept the milk itself, difficulty in keeping everything sterile – we teach that it is still better to continue breastfeeding. I looked at the dilemma facing this mother. If I was the mother, thinking, 'Here I am holding this baby, breastfeeding and I have a 14 per cent chance of transmitting the virus to my baby,' how would I feel? Psychologically, it is killing to the mother."

Mphatso was also aware of the whole area of stigma and discrimination connected with HIV/AIDS. Even though mothers are taught how to lower the risk of transmission, the grandmothers, who often do much of the child-rearing, are usually not aware of their daughter's diagnosis.

Once they know the mother is HIV-positive, she will be discriminated against.

Mphatso says, "I was interested in looking at all that. How does this mother feel? She is in a dilemma. She wants to protect her baby, she wants to protect herself, she wants to do the best she can, but she doesn't have the resources to do what she would like to do. All the issues surrounding the socio-economic status of that woman affect the means she has to protect her baby."

Wanting to examine these issues further, in 2005 Mphatso applied to Queen's University in Belfast to do a Master's in Midwifery, based on the prevention of mother-to-child transmission of HIV/AIDS.

Arriving in Northern Ireland from Malawi, she was initially overwhelmed by the choice of merchandise in the shops and the abundance of personal possessions. She was shocked at the sight of someone throwing away leftover grated cheese because they had not used it all. Coming from a country where having enough food is a daily concern for many people, she found such thoughtless waste unimaginable.

During her year studying in Ireland, she lived on the college campus with other students. She came expecting the cool reception that she had experienced in South Africa and was amazed by the welcoming warmth of the Irish. One of her first experiences was in the computer lab at the college, where she was having some difficulty.

"At that stage I was not using a computer much in Malawi. I didn't know how to go onto email, so I asked one young student if he would help me. I expected him to be rude, thinking, 'What is this old woman trying to do?', but he was so good; he helped me step by step. As I carried on doing all the work that I had to do, he came back and asked, 'Are you OK? If you need any help, please come and ask me.' I couldn't believe it. He was so young and I didn't think he would care so much. He really touched me."

Another day she set out to go to the library at the Royal Victoria Hospital. Stopping a lady weighed down with bags, she asked the way to the correct bus stop. Instead of giving directions, the lady turned and walked with her to the bus stop, declining Mphatso's offer of help with her bags.

"She talked to me while we walked and when we got there she said, 'The bus stops here. It comes every few minutes but even if it is delayed, wait here. It will take you right to the Royal.' That was very special. She could just have given me directions but she walked with me, with all those bags. It amazed me that people were so helpful."

At the weekends Mphatso had the opportunity to visit different churches, telling people in the services about her life and work in Malawi. She enjoyed meeting people from a wide variety of backgrounds and experiencing the oneness in Christ that rises above the difficulties of race, colour, and culture. With a broader view of life and a deeper understanding of the issues surrounding HIV, she returned to Ekwendeni Nursing College as Deputy Principal and Dean of Faculty.

In 2008 she was asked to take over as Director of LISAP. Aware of her inadequacies, but trusting in God to help her, Mphatso accepted. It meant shouldering responsibility for the work of this HIV/AIDS programme throughout the whole northern region of the country.

She quotes their mission statement: "Our mission is co-ordinating, mobilizing and empowering communities to initiate and sustain HIV/AIDS interventions with a Christ-centred spirit." Prevention talks and awareness-raising exercises to help curb the spread of the virus are an important part of the work but prevention is balanced by work on impact mitigation, accepting the fact of HIV in the community, and helping people live positively with the virus. The many people widowed and orphaned as a result of HIV/AIDS across the region need help at different levels. Little ones may be living with a grandmother or other relatives or with infected parents. One avenue of help is to bring them together in a community-based childcare centre, where they can socialize with others and have at least one meal a day.

Mphatso says, "A meal is perhaps just a bowl of porridge, but for some that's all they get. We have what we call a children's corner for six- to eighteen-year-olds. This is like a social treatment centre where trained adults help these children de-stress, talk about their problems and learn to deal with them. They have the opportunity to play and do some crafts to take them out of the daily situation at home and have a different scenario for a while."

LISAP pays school fees for a number of children, although choosing a small number from the hundreds of applicants each year is one of the most difficult decisions Mphatso faces. For some young people, who are beyond school age but have responsibility for their family, vocational skills training is provided in subjects such as carpentry and tailoring. They return to their home village equipped to use these skills to support themselves and their family.

The women's empowerment programme aims to counteract the increased risks of forced marriage for young girls, brought about by the combination of poverty and HIV. Women are taught how savings and loans can enable them to be independent and give them the confidence to withstand pressures from men who carry the risks of HIV/ AIDS. As they learn to save what they have and combine as a group to start small businesses, they realize they are not helpless and do have some measure of control over their own lives.

The programme is also trying to encourage church leaders and traditional leaders to work together in response to HIV/AIDS.

Mphatso is clear. "For so long the church has been silent and left this work to secular organizations. Only when the church brings HIV to the pulpit can we bring the message to everyone. We need to see that these people who are HIV-positive are church members and, if they die, it is the church that is dying. LISAP works with both church and community – we are so much more effective if we work together. Some small churches do not have the capacity to deal with HIV/AIDS, so we need to bring them together with bigger churches that do. That means members from all the churches will be cared for."

The programme encompasses every aspect of life affected by HIV/AIDS in the community. Mphatso emphasizes the ongoing, developing nature of the work.

"Because HIV is dynamic, we need also to be dynamic. We often fail because HIV changes its face all the time. We think, 'We will tackle this, we will tackle that, we are winning.' But there will always be another problem."

She cites the example of the use of antiretroviral drugs to prolong someone's life.

"With the coming of these drugs we think, 'Hallelujah! We have won the battle.' But what comes after this? People taking these drugs need to have plenty of food because the drugs make them sick if they don't have enough to eat. Many of the people we are dealing with don't have money for food, so they will not continue with their treatment unless we are able to provide food alongside the medication."

She is concerned about the enormity of the problem in the country. According to the World Health Organization, two-thirds of all HIV infections are in Sub-Saharan Africa.[1] Around 200,000 people in the north of Malawi are living with HIV, with all the complex needs that the situation entails. Out of a population of 14 million in the country as a whole, almost 1 million people are living with HIV. The leading cause of death among adults, it is a major factor in the country's low life expectancy of just forty-three years.[2] The present economic crisis has had a negative impact, as organizations which might have funded the work of LISAP in the past have become more focused on the universal issue of climate change. Despite the challenges, however, Mphatso turns to her faith in a God who will not let them down.

"All my life has been a life of faith. He continued being faithful to me even when I didn't know him. The situation I work in now, all I am doing, is because of Christ. If it was not for my faith in God, I would have given up a long time ago. In 2 Corinthians 12 Paul says he will boast about his weakness, because all he has done has been because of Christ; Christ's strength is his strength and his weakness becomes strength in Christ. With all the problems we face, I am made strong because of my weaknesses and because of the one who is in me, who is greater than all that is in the world. It is the grace of Christ that enables this work to continue. His grace is sufficient. All is wrapped up in the sufficiency of the grace of God. Romans 12 verse 1 says, 'Give yourself fully to God as a living sacrifice.' By committing myself to Christ himself, as a living sacrifice, it makes everything worthwhile. All this is not about me but about Christ himself."

Mphatso looks down reflectively at her shining high heels and I wonder if she is seeing the little barefoot girl playing in her grandmother's house, longing to go to school.

"Yes, I have come through many difficult situations, but when I look back I can only say, 'God has been very good to me.'"

4
Maria

Leaving the cool quietness of Mphatso's office in LISAP, I step out into the mid-morning sunshine and am immediately caught up in chattering groups of people making their way on foot down the dusty road to the market and the hospital. Grateful for the shade of tall jacaranda trees, spreading their green-leafed branches overhead like elegant parasols, I pass a sign for the Double G's Restaurant. Glory Gondwe's eating establishment is a recent addition to Ekwendeni's attractions.

At the roundabout marking the incongruous concrete apex of Ekwendeni's dirt roads, I meet Barbara, part-time co-ordinator of the local mental health programme and nurse-in-charge of the children's ward at Ekwendeni Hospital. Passionate about helping people with mental health problems, Barbara has been involved in setting up a local non-governmental organization in partnership with the Northern Ireland Association of Mental Health. The programme has made a significant difference to the lives of these often marginalized people, offering assessment, medication, and a support group alongside practical help with daily living, such as fertilizer, clothes, or even a goat.

As part of the programme, Barbara was invited to Belfast to observe how patients were helped there, so she is well equipped for her task today as my guide and translator.

As she gives me the hospital tour, I am struck by a variety of signs ranging from a plaque commemorating the opening of the newer part of the building in 2005 to a banner pinned to one of the outside walls, headed "Cleanliness is Life". The body of the text reminds us to avoid cross-infection by not sitting on beds and to wash hands before and after examining every patient. I wonder if this is directed at staff rather than visitors. Vivid red bougainvillea vines brighten the monochrome hospital paintwork.

We meet up with Maria Silo, who works in the AIDS support programme. I know she is HIV-positive but she looks very healthy to me, and her wide smile indicates her willingness to spend some time with us, talking about her life. Together we make our way through the hospital to the small private wing, where we manage to locate a free room. Closing the door on the busyness of the hospital day, we make ourselves comfortable as Maria recounts the background to her role in the hospital.

With her eyes on the ground, Maria's voice is low as she starts to recall her early years.

"I was born in Zambia because my parents had left Malawi to work there. When my parents divorced, my grandmother came to Zambia to collect me and my sister. I was only three years old when she brought us back to the capital, Lilongwe, where my grandfather worked with the Stagecoach bus company. When he retired six years later, we all moved to Balaka in the south of the country." Maria has long since accepted the disruption of her young life and reports it with equanimity. As she talks about her parents' divorce and the children moving to live with their grandmother, I am getting a sense of déjà vu. How many children's lives in Malawi follow this pattern?

After the divorce, Maria's mother returned to the north of Malawi, while her father remarried and stayed in Zambia. Maria and her sister grew up with their grandparents, accepting the situation but wondering occasionally where their parents were and when they would see them again. The question was answered when Maria's father suddenly arrived one day from Zambia to visit the family in Balaka. He wasted no time in clarifying the reason for his visit.

"My daughters, your grandparents are getting older and less able to care for you. We will go together to Ekwendeni to see your mother." The girls, now teenagers, were delighted to have the opportunity to make the long journey north despite a certain diffidence about seeing their mother again after such a long time. In the event, their mother agreed to keep the two girls, and Maria started at Ekwendeni Primary School in Standard 6.

Settling into life with her mother, Maria completed primary school, but did not think much about any further education. Secondary-school fees would have been prohibitive for her mother and, in any case, she had a feeling that Mr Mponda, who sold bananas in the market, was showing an interest in her. Each time she went to the market, Maria made a point of stopping to buy bananas from him. One day he sent people from his home place to visit Maria's home and ask for the seventeen-year-old in marriage.

The dowry was agreed at twenty-five kwacha and three cows. Together with her aunt, Maria went to her future husband's home to prepare for the "day for advice", which would take place on the third day after her arrival. For the first two days she acted like a visitor, staying in the house, with few people realizing the reason for her presence. The family waited in anticipation for the main day to make it public.

On the day itself, the women of the family gathered. Once Maria had been formally introduced to all the relatives present, her aunt and her husband's relatives took turns to pass on to her the advice traditionally given to all new brides. Coming from far away and unfamiliar with their ways, she needed to be made aware of how life was conducted in the family she was joining. Topics covered included how to look after her new husband, how to organize the household budget, personal cleanliness, living with her in-laws, and living with her neighbours. She was presented with gifts, including money that would be used to help with the cost of the wedding. As with all celebrations, singing and dancing were an integral part of the proceedings.

A few days later, the wedding itself took place. Mr Mponda and his family sat outside on the ground. Maria sat on a special mat, in a suitable aspect of submission, her head covered with a *chitenge*. After a respectful interval, the groom's family came forward, laid the dowry money on the mat beside her, and removed the *chitenge* from her head. Maria rose from her mat, cooked a big pot of *nsima*, and served it to the extended family. Afterwards she washed the plates, talked to the visitors, and tidied up the house. With the traditional ceremony completed, she was now free to attend to all the daily duties of the home. She was wife to Mr Mponda, whom she would continue to address by his surname as a mark of respect.

After the marriage, the couple moved to live in Salima in central Malawi, where Maria's husband had started working with the agricultural department. In the following years, four children were born there, one girl and three boys. In 1992, having begun to attend the local church, they decided to have their marriage blessed in church and the children baptized. The following year the family moved again, this time back to Lilongwe, where Maria had lived as a young child with her grandparents. Maria looks back on the simple contentment of this stage of her life, when she was unaware of all that was to come.

"I was just living quietly at home, looking after the house and my children while my husband was working. Then my mother became sick with breast cancer. We brought her to Lilongwe Hospital where she had surgery, and we hoped she would recover. My sister and brother were in Ekwendeni, so I cared for her alone in Lilongwe. Unfortunately her condition deteriorated; they told us she had come too late and she died within a short time. She had married again in Ekwendeni and had a six-month-old baby, so when she was dying she left the child with me." Maria gives a heavy sigh as she recalls the sorrow of losing the mother with whom she had been reunited after all their years apart.

Mr Mponda was now working as a driver. One weekend his boss came to ask him to accompany him on a special job. They left together on a Saturday, but by the Sunday he had not returned. Already concerned that something was wrong, Maria was apprehensive when people arrived unexpectedly at her house on Monday. Gradually they broke the news that her husband had been involved in a car accident. Together with her husband's relatives, she travelled to Likuni, where the accident was said to have taken place.

Seeing people along the roadside, they asked, "Have you heard about a car accident near here?"

"No," they replied, "but what we have heard is that people were fighting in a car over there."

Unsure what this meant, the family found the site of the accident, to be told by local people that the driver had died. Others said he had been injured and taken to hospital. Hoping for the best, they made their way to Lilongwe Hospital but a search of the wards proved fruitless. Moving on to the mortuary, they were faced with rows of bodies waiting for identification and collection. Suddenly Maria recognized her husband's shoes – his body was beyond recognition. She realized that, whatever had happened in the car, he was now lying in the mortuary; he had gone.

Shock shielded Maria from the immediate impact of his death. She was in denial, not willing to accept that her husband was dead, despite having seen it with her own eyes. Four months pregnant with another child, she went through the motions of the burial process at his home in Zomba.

Mr Mponda's death ushered in a time of great struggle for Maria. Her husband had always been the breadwinner and provided for the needs of the children while she stayed at home to care for them. Aware that she now had to find money so that her family could eat, Maria did what she could, selling sugar cane, avocados, and sweets. At least there were no school fees to pay because the children were still young, in primary school and nursery.

For the first few months, not knowing what else to do, Maria remained with her in-laws, glad of their help in supporting the family. Once her baby was born, however, she had a desire to return to her home in Ekwendeni. The family agreed, although, before she left, her husband's sisters came and took her only daughter to live with them in Zomba, where she could help them in the home. Maria had no choice but to give her up because she knew she was struggling to support the children on her own. It was one less child to feed, and her aunts would care for her.

Shortly after she arrived in Ekwendeni, Maria began to feel unwell. She developed shingles and in the course of her hospital treatment she was tested for HIV. After an anxious three-day wait, she was given the dreaded news – she was positive.

"It was not easy being told that result. At first I was shocked and upset but then I thought, 'What can I do, since my husband is already dead? Who can I blame?' So I just decided to accept the situation. He died in the car accident in 1996 and I discovered I had HIV in 1998, so there was no way to check if he was positive."

Although Maria was HIV-positive, the virus had not yet developed into AIDS. She was fortunate to be one of the first to be given antiretroviral drugs, which interfere with the reproduction of the virus in the body. From time to time she developed various infections as her body fought the virus, but on the whole she managed to remain healthy enough to care for her family. It can take up to ten years for an HIV-infected person to develop AIDS; antiretroviral drugs can slow down the process even further.

The following year, her youngest son, now three years old, also became unwell. He had a nasty cough that refused to clear up, had lost his appetite, and was losing weight. Eventually it was discovered he had tuberculosis, often an HIV-related infection. It is estimated that one-third of the 40 million people living with HIV/AIDS worldwide are co-infected with tuberculosis.[1] A test soon proved that he was indeed HIV-positive. He also would need to take antiretrovirals.

The other children all tested negative. Maria reflects on the implications of the test results.

"One possibility is that the other children were born when both of us as parents were negative. When my husband got the driving job, he went backwards and forwards to Mozambique transporting people; perhaps he had other relationships when he was travelling, got infected, and then brought the virus back home. I could have passed it on to my son in childbirth or when breastfeeding."

Faced with the news, Maria tried to take her diagnosis as positively as possible, knowing she had no option but to accept it. Refusing to hide from the matter, she began to share with people that she was HIV-positive. In 1999 her sister also tested positive but she reacted very differently, and Maria watched the struggles she went through in her denial of the situation. Not long after receiving the news her sister died, leaving a child who was the next to become Maria's responsibility.

She now had her sister's and mother's children as well as her own to care for. With her health reasonably stable, she did everything she could think of to raise money, selling eggs and water to passengers at bus stops, even breaking stones for the new road that was being built locally. She wanted to do her best for the children.

Life was difficult, however, and in 2000, when she met a man who was HIV-positive and who offered her the opportunity to marry again, she seized on it as a solution to her problems, giving her the support that she needed. Little did she realize how dangerous it would be for her. She became pregnant, which lowered her immunity and left her open to a complexity of infections. Her baby was stillborn; shortly afterwards, her husband also died. They had been together for only one year. She could not believe she had lost so many people in her life: two husbands, her sister, her mother, the baby.

She became very ill with constant vomiting and diarrhoea and was incontinent for a year. The traumatic experience of that time remained with her as a constant reminder of the different life she was now leading.

"I learned a hard lesson, which I was able to pass on to others. Once you discover you have HIV it is no good marrying or becoming pregnant. My husband knew I was positive, but he was already positive himself so we thought we could support each other. I thought I was solving a problem, not knowing I was adding to it."

Our interview is interrupted by the musical tones of her mobile phone. She glances at it and turns it off. In the midst of the searing tragedies of life in this country, I allow myself a quiet smile at the co-existence of contrasting cultures.

When Maria became unwell, Ekwendeni Hospital was her lifeline, providing her with the essential antiretroviral (ARV) drugs that she needed. Too sick to work, she approached the hospital AIDS programme for support. Christian friends from the local church came with food to help her.

At one stage, when she was very ill, local people set her house on fire, fearful of her illness and wanting to get rid of her. Shirley and Marion, missionaries who lived nearby, helped her rebuild the house.

She reflects, "We did not even know each other well at that stage but they came alongside me to help with Christian love. The family had so many different needs and I had no way of supplying those needs myself when I was ill. Every day we needed to eat, to buy food, to buy fertilizer for the garden so we could grow some food ourselves. My situation would have been desperate without outside support, but many people helped in different ways. I thank God for all those who were so kind and who show God's love still."

She is amazed how God took care of her when she needed it most. Just at the time when her children reached the age for secondary school, she met Jim and Ruth, a couple who were visiting Ekwendeni from Ireland. Touched by her story, they paid the necessary school fees for the children.

Many people from Scotland and Ireland contributed and assisted her from that time onwards.

She says, "One minister from Scotland organized a group of people who bought the medicine every month for me and for others. These ARV drugs made me feel a lot better. The only reason I am still alive is the support I have received with the drugs and the love and care of these people, many of whom I have never met. Once in a while I am unwell, but generally I am fine. If I need something I know I can go to Mphatso at LISAP for help, or Esther Lupafya, who co-ordinates the hospital AIDS programme. Douglas Lungu, who used to be in charge of the hospital at Ekwendeni, has now moved to Lilongwe but I can still go to him for advice and he has been very supportive."

Because historically HIV/AIDS has largely been a taboo subject, with discrimination common, few people living with the virus have been willing to talk about their status. When Maria began to let it be known that she was HIV-positive, she was invited to talk to others affected by the virus. In 2003 she was officially employed by the hospital AIDS programme. Now she works in providing home-based care, listening to patients, sharing her story, and reassuring them that they too can live positively with AIDS.

Although there is no cure for HIV, consistent use of antiretroviral treatment, together with good nutrition and a healthy lifestyle, can greatly slow the progression of the virus in the body and help maintain a high quality of life. Until 2003, the high cost of the medicines prevented their widespread use in many countries. But, in recent years, increased political and financial commitment has dramatically expanded access to HIV therapy.

Last year Maria's daughter made the journey home to her mother in Ekwendeni from the south of the country, and was admitted to Ekwendeni Hospital, very ill. A short time later she died there, leaving a young granddaughter with Maria and continuing the cycle of grandmother care. At forty-two years old, Maria has seen a world of illness and death but has come through with resilience and hope. As soon as she hears of anyone who needs her support, she is at their home.

She says, "In addition to the drugs, people with HIV often need a listening ear and individual support. I do not hesitate to go, because I know how I have been supported and assisted by many people. I share my story and encourage people to be positive as they look forward to the rest of their lives. I tell them there are thousands of people with AIDS and many are leading full and productive lives. They can do the same. I try to encourage them to accept the diagnosis, to be aware of the treatment and help that is available, to look forward with hope, to be faithful to one another and support each other."

Maria is very grateful to those who come to Malawi, whether to work for a longer time or just on a short visit, who help in so many ways, both material and spiritual. She is aware that there are many people she has never met who pray for her and send help, not only for her but for many others also, because her story is only one among many.

A smile lights up her face as she articulates the reason for her hope. "My faith has become stronger after seeing what God can do and how he can help through other people. I tell others to believe in God because he is with them always, all the time. He is there, aware of their problems. He answers, he heals, he provides."

I say my farewells to Maria and Barbara and am glad of some time to myself as I make my way back along the paths to Helen and Robin's house, caught up in the emotion of all that I have heard in the past few days. Overwhelmed by the trials faced by people in their everyday lives, I am comforted to see African and European taking on these challenges together, with the love of Christ that overcomes all cultural barriers shining through. This was my final visit in Ekwendeni. Tomorrow we will head south.

5
Kondwani

"Listen to that singing!" As we drive past the church on Saturday, I roll down the car window and lean out to see what is going on. A group of girls in blue uniforms stand in an informal circle, singing with enthusiastic abandon. The African harmonies rise on the morning air, lifting our spirits as we get out of the car to take advantage of the spontaneous performance. It turns out to be the local Girls' Brigade, waiting for transport to the GB International Day of Prayer. On the other side of the church, the Boys' Brigade, in their smart blue caps and white shirts, are also gathering in excited anticipation of a day out. We take final photographs of Ekwendeni and set off on the road to Mzuzu and then south-east towards Lake Malawi.

Our plan is to have an overnight stop halfway down the western shore of the lake, before continuing on to Blantyre. The third largest lake in Africa at 580 kilometres long, Lake Malawi runs along the eastern border of the country for almost its entire length and is a favourite stop for travellers. A scenic drive from Mzuzu through valleys and past mountains brings us to the town of Nkhata Bay on the edge of the lake, and we turn southwards. Very soon we realize that, rather than running along the lakeside, the road is just far enough from the water to obscure the picturesque view we were anticipating when we planned our route.

We find our entertainment instead in the variety of produce for sale along the way – bananas hanging from tall stands, locally made footballs held high by young people as we drive through a rubber plantation, piles of small fish displayed along the roadside where it runs closer to the lake. Bicycles predominate over cars on the road; we pass a number of hardy tourists identifying with the local mode of transport, with all the necessities for their trip strapped to their bicycles. I wonder how far they are intending to cycle and what experiences face them along the way.

Spotting a sign for the Chinteche Inn, we follow a narrow road down to the edge of the lake, where we stop for lunch. The sand is a soft, white carpet between our toes, the water cool and clear, the sun warm on our faces. We eat looking out over the lake and the almost deserted beach. If we didn't have a schedule to keep and the rest of the journey in front of us, it would be tempting to go no further.

However, we have places to be. Not far along the road we come to Old Bandawe, where the graves of the first missionaries line the shore of the lake. The long row of headstones stands as a permanent symbol of the cost of bringing the gospel to the country.

We read the inscriptions.

"In loving memory of James Edward Fraser of Glasgow, Scotland. Born 19th January 1874. Died 28th March 1899."

"In memory of James Sutherland, who died Sept. 29th 1885, aged 26 years."

The lettering on some of the headstones is almost impossible to make out, but we note that women and children are buried alongside the men, all presumably having submitted to malaria or blackwater fever. We stand in silence, touched by the dedication and commitment of these young lives.

As we leave, we pass Old Bandawe Church, in the grounds of which another group of young people are expressing their faith in enthusiastic song and dance. The sacrifice has not been in vain.

As we travel southwards, the landscape flattens out. We drive through sugar cane and across single-lane bridges. Throughout the journey we have been on the watch for a petrol station with fuel. Since our arrival in Malawi, a fuel shortage has resulted in long queues at petrol stations, especially when word gets out that fuel has arrived. A fire extinguisher prominently displayed on the forecourt warns motorists that petrol pumps are empty. Driving through the Dwangwa Sugar Estate, we suddenly come upon a filling station minus a fire extinguisher. With no queue in evidence, we are doubtful of success, but pull in anyway and are pleasantly surprised to be able to fill our petrol tank. It is a relief to have the fuel needed for the next leg of the journey.

We arrive at Nkhotakota potteries, where we are delighted to find we are booked into a small chalet on the edge of the beach. Hot after our journey, it is not long before we are luxuriating in the refreshing waters of the lake. Dusk falls before six o'clock as usual, and we eat outside, to the sound of water lapping softly on the shore. As we wander back to our chalet, gentle waves reflect ribbons of moonlight across the surface of the lake. The peace and beauty of our overnight stop throw into relief much of what we have seen and heard over the preceding days. I appreciate the break from the intensity of shared emotions.

During the night a storm blows up. Waking to a level of noise justifying a hurricane, we quickly peer outside to inspect the damage. Amazingly, while there seems little effect on land, the lake has been transformed since yesterday. Blue has turned to a metallic grey and waves pound the shore with the power of some demonic machine. It is the water, rather than wind, that is creating the noise.

Fascinating though the lake is in its different moods, we have a journey to make before evening. With a brief stop to admire the attractive ceramics in the pottery, we set off southwards once more. Items for sale at the roadside have graduated from foodstuffs to charcoal and for a short distance we follow a bus with a sign emblazoned across the back: "In Jesus we trust". Presumably they feel he is more reliable than the vehicle.

In the town of Salima we make a recommended stop for ice cream. A map of Africa on the wall proclaims, "Ice Cream Den. The only place in Africa where you can have delicious food." We retire to the shady tables outside to enjoy this unique experience.

Back on the road, baobabs, the famous "upside-down" trees, alternate with mosques to relieve the barren landscape. Suddenly driving becomes more hazardous as we come upon a succession of busy villages packed with pedestrians, goats, chickens, and an increasing number of bicycles. The latter transport not only humans, but sheets of corrugated iron, long bundles of grass for roofing material, firewood stacked tall behind the cyclist, and huge bags of grain or tobacco. I count eight heavy stalks of sugar cane, at least two and a half metres long, protruding on either side of a bicycle weaving its way precariously through people and animals. We reach the town of Zomba with a certain sense of achievement at not having collided with any of these obstacles.

In Zomba we break our journey to visit the theological college, where many of the Malawian church ministers train, and meet the vice-principal, Revd Vaseline Mwale. Unfortunately, time, and the state of the road, prevents us from driving up to the plateau, where the promise of beautiful views over the countryside sounds very tempting.

Arriving in Blantyre before nightfall, we suddenly find ourselves in rush-hour traffic, a shock after the lack of cars up to this point. We check into our accommodation and discover we can get internet access. We send off some emails to reassure the family that we're still alive, enjoy our evening meal, and make arrangements to visit the government-run Queen Elizabeth Hospital the next day.

The sound of singing becomes louder as we follow Dr Neil Kennedy, a consultant paediatrician from Northern Ireland, along the hospital corridor.

"Is there a service taking place somewhere in the hospital?" I ask. Neil looks over his shoulder.

"No, we're being pursued by a body," he replies. I look at him quizzically, and then follow his gaze. Behind us an inert figure on a hospital bed is being wheeled down the corridor, surrounded by a crowd of singing women.

"When someone dies, members of the family take the body from the ward and escort it to the mortuary, singing hymns as they go. This is one of the children from the ward we visited."

We have just left a ward of malnourished children. In the past, Neil explains, children tended to be malnourished owing to a lack of protein in their diet, arriving at the hospital with the tell-tale signs of kwashiorkor, distended bellies and matted hair. These days, with an adequate food supply in Malawi, this is rarely the case. Young children now presenting with malnourishment tend to have been born HIV-positive. One fifteen-month-old sits quietly on his mother's lap. He looks barely half that age.

"About 20 per cent of these children will die," Neil tells us. "The rest will recover with treatment and go back home." It means that some days he will lose four or five children – on a bad day it could be as many as sixteen.

"That's tough," he admits. "And the day you stop finding it tough is the day you shouldn't be here."

Attached to this ward is a unit with a row of rectangular wooden boxes on a wide shelf. In fact they are little cots, each containing a tiny sick baby, some with tubes attached. This is an ICU for the very young children. The mothers also sit in a row, one at the end of each cot. One child, looking slightly more alive than the others, is being nursed by his mother. He has been here for the last two months.

Most of the children seem to have family around them. We move across to the ward for slightly older children and pause at a sign on the door of ICU: "Only one visitor per bed". As we open the door, we are met by a mass of people and noise. One bed has about ten people round it. The child has come in with a serious head injury.

In the Accident and Emergency Department, around 300 children are seen each morning. On the wall a poster depicts various types of child abuse, part of the all-important awareness-raising programme.

Leaving the wards, we move to the staff canteen where, over lunch, Neil tells us more about his work at the hospital.

"Everywhere in Sub-Saharan Africa has seen a huge rise in abuse cases in recent years. When I first came to Malawi in 1997, people claimed they had very little problem with child abuse, but awareness has gradually increased."

Soon after he arrived, Neil saw a ten-year-old girl who had a sexually transmitted infection. She had been sent to the hospital by the village healer.

"What did the village healer say to you?" he asked the father.

"He said he thought someone had slept with my daughter."

"He was right," Neil tells us. "That was exactly the problem, and it is happening all the time."

Over the years, doctors in the hospital saw an increasing number of children who had been abused. Around 2006, they started giving them anti-AIDS drugs as a preventative measure.

Neil says, "When we started doing this, we were seeing about four or five children a month, but the numbers began to increase and by the time I arrived at Queen Elizabeth in 2008 we were seeing about fifteen a month. I remember seeing three kids in one night who had all been raped."

Families of these children come to the hospital for a variety of reasons, but top of the list is probably access to HIV drugs. To come, however, is not an easy decision, Neil explains.

"There is a balance between telling and not telling. There is enormous pressure on children not to tell about abuse because of the stigma and feelings of shame, guilt, and fear, especially if it's an uncle or dad who is involved. There are huge economic repercussions for the family: Dad is going to be arrested; the family is going to be ousted from the family home; everyone will be destitute. One reason for telling, on the other hand, is the possibility of contracting HIV. Parents, increasingly aware of the possibility that their children might be HIV-positive as a result of sexual contact, will bring them for treatment. It's much easier for us to give drugs to prevent a child getting HIV – parents are very grateful. If they test negative, it is not so easy to persuade parents that no treatment is needed."

Alongside his work in child protection, Neil is involved in many different aspects of hospital life, including teaching every medical student in the country.

He says, "I have never worked as hard in my life as I have over the last few years, but it is tremendously fulfilling to feel you are contributing more than just service delivery. The great thing is that we can bring the gospel into our daily lives in the hospital. There is no objection to faith-based groups being involved; we start many of our meetings with prayer and I pray regularly with some of my trainees and talk openly with patients about how they are doing spiritually."

The opportunity to deliver talks and host events for the student-led Student Christian Movement opens up more direct contact with Christian students. Later in the year, Neil plans to take a team of students and doctors to Embangweni, exposing them to life in rural Malawi.

"Eighty per cent of people in Malawi live in rural areas but most of the medical students are fairly middle class, coming from a background where the family has been able to afford the fees for secondary school and university. Mostly from urban areas, they find it difficult to understand the need in rural parts of the country."

Neil continues his explanation as he conducts us through the hospital compound towards the students' halls of residence. "The government try to encourage young doctors to consider going to a rural hospital but the problem is, when they go there, they find they are perhaps the only doctor for a couple of hundred thousand people and have to cope with all their own administration as well as the clinical demands. A twenty-four-year-old who just wants to be a doctor suddenly finds himself swamped with administration, attending meetings, perhaps contending with a hospital matron who is twice his age, perhaps facing corruption in the system; it can all become too much pressure. They want to be doctors, they don't want to be administrators; they are far too young to be administrators and so they tend to stay maybe a year or two and then leave as soon as possible."

Having arrived at some smart buildings immediately identifiable as student halls of residence, Neil leaves us in the care of Kondwani Zgambo, a second-year medical student, who welcomes us to his room. Pointing out the study area and noticeboard covered in photographs and memorabilia, he offers us a seat and perches on the edge of the patchwork quilt that covers his bed. For a moment, facing this articulate young man in his sweatshirt and blue jeans, I feel I could be talking to a student anywhere in the world. He informs us that his name means "Be happy".

"I was born in 1984 – I'm a bit old," he says apologetically. He doesn't look old to me, but I suppose twenty-seven is older than most second-year students. Resting his arms on his knees, he clasps his hands together and leans forward as he talks.

"My father was married. When his first wife died young, leaving two small children, he married my mother, who then had five children," Kondwani explains. "We are all from the same father so we are a family of seven children." With his parents struggling to make ends meet as subsistence farmers, Kondwani walked a long distance to primary school, sometimes on an empty stomach, but the lack of money spurred him on to work harder at school. His first two brothers had not stayed in school, because of the death of their mother, so he considered it an achievement when he made it through primary school to Standard 8.

"My dad kept on saying, 'You need to work hard if things are to get better for you and for those who come behind you.'" He pauses to offer further explanation. "I am the first born to my mother, so I feel that responsibility.

Even when I was too young to really understand what was happening, I remember my mother kneeling down and praying very much for me and for us all, that we would work hard. She always encouraged us to go to school."

Failing to gain admission to a government secondary school, Kondwani ended up going to a community school, where he quickly realized the standard was not what he wanted. The only alternative was to try to obtain enough money to pay for one of the more affordable private schools.

His parents, convinced of the importance of education, were keen to help as much as possible, but it was a constant struggle to support the whole family. Having chosen a boarding school that he thought would better meet his needs, Kondwani worked with a determination that brought him to the attention of the headmaster. Impressed by this enthusiastic young student, each time there was a problem with school fees during his first two years at the school, the headmaster informed his tobacco-growing parents that they could pay after the harvest. Kondwani felt that God was watching over him.

"That does not normally happen with fees; I just saw the hand of the Lord in it. At that time tobacco sales were good, although they decreased later; it worked out well for me at that stage." Global health concerns about smoking did not occur to him; he was focused on the only means of survival known to the family.

The following year, however, with the fall-off in demand for tobacco and the resulting lack of income, life became more difficult. He was one of two students who passed with high marks at the end of Form 2, but there were no fees for him to start Form 3. His parents suggested he stay at home for a year while they gathered fees together, but, knowing how difficult it would be to pick up his studies again after a break, Kondwani was reluctant to do this. He went from contact to contact, explaining their difficulties as a family and trying to borrow money that his parents could repay later.

Unsuccessful in all these attempts, Kondwani went to school to alert his friends to his difficulties. Somehow the news that he was going to have to drop out found its way to the headmaster, who was horrified. "We can't allow that," he said. "You've been one of the top students over the past year. Just come to school, and when your parents get money they can pay."

Again Kondwani felt God's hand on the situation, knowing it was very unusual to be allowed to attend without fees being paid up front. He returned to school feeling positive, but realized once he was there that he had nothing to live on as a boarder.

"I remember there was a time I even had to sell my clothes to other students to get some money. The headmaster had told me not to worry about the fees, but I had no money for anything else that I needed to live, even things like sugar to put in my tea. Thank God – he took care of me and brought me through. I just made sure I kept my hard-working spirit and made the most of the chance to be there in school."

At the end of secondary school, Kondwani did not manage to gain entrance to the government university. Instead, he was offered a place in the Malawian College of Health Sciences in Lilongwe, a government college that trains clinical officers. The latter play a key role in the medical work in African countries, carrying out many of the tasks of doctors in diagnosis and treatment, but with a shorter, less expensive period of training. Kondwani was reluctant to accept the offer, insisting that he wanted a degree, not a diploma. His parents, however, were realistic. "You'd better just go to college when you have a place. Don't turn down the opportunity."

With a heavy heart, he took their advice. In the course of his first year he met students from the college of medicine in the hospital, and every time it happened he was conscious of a pang in his heart. He really wanted to be a doctor, not a clinical officer.

"I vowed to myself, 'I will not die a clinical officer.' That drove me on. When I met medical students in the corridor and we shared things together, I came away inspired. I joined the Christian Medical Fellowship, where I met Christian doctors and medical students and had the opportunity to discuss with them the interaction of faith and medicine. How do we handle situations we meet in the hospital as Christian medics? That was very important to me and helped a great deal."

At night he prayed that somehow God would intervene and allow him to upgrade from the clinical officer's course to study medicine. He knew his parents would not easily accept a decision to spend more time studying instead of starting work straight away.

Entrance qualifications were the problem; in order to gain admission to the government university, he needed to improve his secondary-school grades. Faced with this challenge, Kondwani devised a strategy. Making a survey of all first-year clinical officer students, he enquired how many of them would like to be doctors. Three from the year responded in the affirmative. They agreed to work together to improve their school grades while they were still fresh from secondary school, encouraging each other to work harder so that when they finished their clinical officer training they could apply to the University College of Medicine.

Realizing it would be difficult to keep both courses going, they began by obtaining the current secondary-school syllabus. Before long, however, Kondwani's plan foundered as his friends struggled and then abandoned the effort to maintain their first-year college work alongside preparation for retaking secondary-school examinations.

But Kondwani was persistent. "I kept telling myself that it was possible and prayed for God to keep me strong and help me do my best. I was all alone in my determination to continue."

Despite all his hard work, Kondwani almost missed the chance to sit the secondary-school examinations at the end of the year. Setting out on the journey to pay the admission fee, he ran out of transport and had to walk for three hours to get there. With relief, he managed to reach the office before it closed, and complete the necessary documentation.

At the end of the first year of clinical officer training, twenty-one of the 140 students passed the examinations at the first try. Kondwani was one of them.

"That was like a testimony to me because, as well as

being part of that twenty-one, I had achieved what I wanted. I had the necessary secondary-school grades in physics and additional maths to qualify me to go to university. I was the only person in that big hall who was taking the additional maths examination. I remember the invigilator asking me, 'Why do you want to do that?' I said, 'I want to be a doctor.'"

His initial plan was to finish the three years of clinical officer training before applying for medical college. At the end of his second year, unable to control his impatience, he decided to test the water by applying early and was thrilled to be offered a place to study medicine. He resolved to abandon clinical officer training and start his medical course immediately.

It was not a straightforward decision. Friends asked him, "Why don't you finish your clinical officer training first, so you can get a qualification that will let you work and have a salary?" But his room-mate's comment encouraged him. "If God has given you a place on that course and he wants you there, there is no way he will fail to provide the fees."

At the time, the cost of the pre-med year, the entry year for the course, was 300,000 kwacha. This was a daunting sum for someone from Kondwani's background. "My parents had never handled 10,000 kwacha in their lives, never mind 100,000. I was relying on a miracle to allow me to pursue my dream."

Confident that the God who had given him the place there would somehow provide his fees, Kondwani set out from Lilongwe to Blantyre University. When he arrived, he had 1,000 kwacha in his pocket. He saw people paying

The road through Ekwendeni gives a panoramic view over northern Malawi.

Joy Mzinza, visiting in Robin and Helen's house, shares her story as a widow in Malawi.

Even in the remote village of Euthini, we are invited to connect and recharge our mobile phones.

Marcus and his brother made and fired the bricks for his new house from local ant-hill clay.

Inside the house Marcus and I sit on upended beehives to talk about his life.

World economics and the international anti-smoking lobby are encouraging the world's most tobacco-dependent country towards diversification.

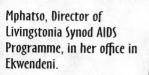

Mphatso, Director of Livingstonia Synod AIDS Programme, in her office in Ekwendeni.

Glory Gondwe's restaurant is Ekwendeni's latest eating establishment.

At Ekwendeni Hospital, Maria shares her experience with others and encourages them to live positively with AIDS.

Lake Malawi offers Brian a welcome break from driving.

Missionary graves at Old Bandawe, a permanent symbol of the cost of bringing the gospel to Malawi.

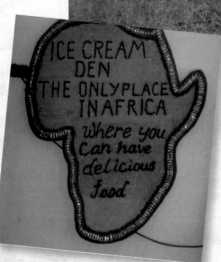

ICE CREAM DEN THE ONLY PLACE IN AFRICA where you can have delicious food

Our much-appreciated ice-cream stop on the road to Blantyre.

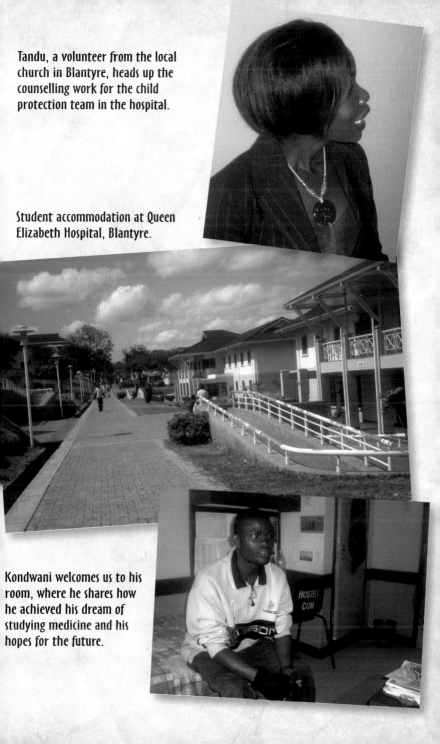

Tandu, a volunteer from the local church in Blantyre, heads up the counselling work for the child protection team in the hospital.

Student accommodation at Queen Elizabeth Hospital, Blantyre.

Kondwani welcomes us to his room, where he shares how he achieved his dream of studying medicine and his hopes for the future.

Sarah and Jimnah work together to offer love and care to the children in Joy Children's Home in Ruiru, Kenya.

With Kasoni in Nairobi, learning something of the cost of standing against Female Genital Mutilation.

On the Mombasa–Malindi road, the roofs of small mud houses provide a template for the soaring thatched hotel roofs nearby.

The dirt road from Malindi to Galana demands certain driving skills . . .

. . . and continues on into the distance for mile after mile.

Mary and I enjoy our picnic on the bank of the Galana river.

The school at Bombi, Galana, offers education to those on both sides of the river.

The Galana bridge enables people to cross without fear of attack from hippo or crocodile.

Saying farewell to our friends in Galana, with Guyo and Naomi on my left.

money and asked the matron where to register.

Indicating the appropriate desk, she said, "Pay your fees there and you will get keys to your room after you've paid."

"How much are the fees?" Kondwani asked, although he had a good idea.

"Three hundred thousand," she replied crisply. There was no way out. Kondwani explained that he did not have the fees. She directed him to the registrar.

"The college is not prepared to help needy students," was his unsympathetic response.

Eventually Kondwani was given keys on a temporary basis and told that he was pre-registered but that if he did not manage to source the money soon, he would have to leave. He discovered there were a number who did not have the required fees.

Gradually students began to be offered various scholarships. One day Kondwani was called to the registrar's office, to be told there was a scholarship available from a Presbyterian church in the United States which was partnering with the Presbyterian Church in Malawi. They wanted to help church hospitals by supporting medical students through their training, on the understanding that they would work in a rural church hospital when they qualified. Kondwani knew that many doctors did not want to work in rural areas because of the challenges it entailed, but he thought, "Maybe this is where God wants me to work, in a mission hospital. I grew up in a small village; I was used to living without all the things people have in town. Perhaps I would be qualified to work in a rural area." Deciding he would welcome the opportunity to go back into the kind of setting he had come from, he gratefully accepted the scholarship.

Kondwani praises God for the help that came in this way. For the past three years, his fees have been paid, without the anxiety of searching for them term by term. Because of his clinical officer training, he is able to work at the church hospital in the rural area of Embangweni during university holidays, receiving an allowance from his sponsors towards food and upkeep.

At the end of his first year, after a series of mishaps including being given the wrong date for the examinations, he failed by one mark.

"That was a very hard moment for me. Eventually I accepted that some things come because God wants to teach us a lesson through them. I had to repeat my first year. But now I'm about to finish my second year, and doing well."

Financial concerns, however, are never far away.

"Currently my family situation is difficult – when anything happens at home they telephone me and the little I get here I have to share with them. I need to send money for my parents and school fees for my brothers and sisters. My mum just called me a short time ago for money for my brother and sister in secondary school. All of them are looking to me, so it will be tough until I graduate. At least when I start to get a salary it will be easier.

"God is taking care of us and there is hope. When I look back at the journey I've made, from where I've come from to where I am now, I realize he has greater plans for me. My dream is to become a great surgeon in Malawi. God tells us in the book of Jeremiah chapter 1:

*"Before I formed you in the womb I knew you,
before you were born I set you apart."'*

I believe that whatever I pass through, it will be turned to joy tomorrow. There is no testimony without trial."

Throughout his time at university, Kondwani has appreciated all the support offered to Christian students. When he got to know Dr Kennedy, he was delighted to realize he had worked in Embangweni, before coming to Blantyre.

"When I came here, the Christian Medical Fellowship was a great support. Meeting people like Dr Kennedy and the team has been amazing. He has been my mentor but he has also become like my spiritual father. I remember one time when I was having problems, he told me, 'Kondwani, don't worry; this is not the end of the road. Keep on pressing forward.' His life has been such an encouragement to me, especially as he spent time in the rural area of Embangweni, where many people do not like to work. He is leading us in an outreach to Embangweni later in the year.

"We need to have a heart to serve others, to see it as a calling. If all of us run away from those places, then who is going to help them? If all of us had that attitude of mission, then the country would be different. If at least some of us have the heart to say, 'Let us go to those places,' then it *will* make a difference. I am really up for that."

With our hearts touched by the staunch dedication of this young man, we pause to pray with him before we part. As he in turn prays spontaneously for us, we feel humbled and blessed by his strong faith, his concern for others, and his commitment to keep following God, wherever he leads. We leave with renewed hope for the future of this country; young people such as this hold the key to a bright tomorrow.

6
Tandu and Chiyembekezo

"Recently I saw a little girl of eight who was admitted with meningitis. We automatically test everyone for HIV. The mother was HIV-negative but the child was positive. There was no other possible explanation but that the child was positive because of sexual contact."

Neil is giving us more background to his child protection work at the hospital.

"The father told the mother he was negative and, because of patient confidentiality, I could not divulge the fact that he was in fact positive and the likely perpetrator. Yet we had to ensure the child was safe. Those are the dilemmas we face."

Neil is about to introduce us to a young teenager who is willing to share her story and the counsellor who has been working with her. I ask him how the present child protection system at the hospital came about.

"Because of the growing number of child abuse cases, I met with the Director of UNICEF and the Malawian Head of Social Welfare. The latter was in tears as I related some of the stories of the children we were seeing. We decided to bring together a number of bodies – UNICEF, juvenile justice, social welfare, the police – to begin providing a child protection service at the hospital."

Neil details the problems. "One factor we were struggling with was a lack of co-ordination between the various people a child might deal with when reporting abuse – clear lines of communication and areas of responsibility were needed. The other factor was the reliability of the story. Doctors didn't know if the story they had heard, which was maybe that the garden boy from next door had leapt over the wall and done it, was really the true story or maybe just a more acceptable story to tell. Perhaps they were sending children back into an abusive situation, with nobody there to stop it. There was no counselling service available, although doctors were very aware of the psychological and health consequences for the rest of a child's life, especially in cases of repeated abuse, if it was not dealt with at the time."

They started to put a team together, including victim support officers. UNICEF were already training care teams who could offer the victims support and a sympathetic ear rather than recrimination. Social welfare provided a specialist social worker, trained and employed to focus solely on child protection issues. On the legal side, they also needed trained and specialist police officers.

A local church saw the need and provided counselling volunteers who were trained and vetted by social welfare. This enabled the setting up of a counselling service at the hospital so that children could be given a follow-up counselling appointment when they first came for help.

Neil brings us up to date with the current situation.

"Now a team of police, social welfare, and counsellors all work together. When a child comes today to Accident and Emergency, a form is completed, with all the details including the medical side of things and the whole story as far as it has been reported. The social worker acts as the co-ordinator, contacting the police to let them know what has happened at the hospital and checking that the police are following up the case. He also contacts the volunteer child protection workers, provided by the government, who go into the community and talk to people in their homes. The counselling service now has its own counselling room where people feel secure. About a third of the children come back for the counselling service, some just once or twice, some multiple times."

Neil is ever more aware of the need for these systems. "It is good to see a more joined-up approach coming together and, when it works, it works really well, but there are still huge numbers of children affected that we never see."

Recent money from UNICEF now allows the social worker and support officers to go out in a vehicle and visit families in their homes to check how things are. If the team suspect that a close family member has maybe committed the abuse but they are not getting that story, at least turning up at the home hopefully acts as some kind of a deterrent.

Neil guides us along hospital paths to the area where a new one-stop centre is being built, funded by UNICEF, to facilitate the multi-disciplinary approach.

He explains, "Different countries do it in different ways, but in Malawi we have decided to put a one-stop centre here in the hospital. Children come to us because of the medical problem and it is good to be able to help them medically and prescribe anti-HIV drugs, but that does not deal with the whole nightmare scenario they are involved in. The centre will facilitate everyone working together. One aim is to record the child's story so that it can be used in court, rather than the child having to repeat the story on multiple occasions."

With the building almost at ceiling height, the one-stop centre is an extensive structure. The scaffolding of slender tree branches raises its arms like an arthritic skeleton alongside the solid brickwork, but the builders are pushing ahead in the hope of having it ready for use within a few months.

"Working with people like Tandu is brilliant. She is sent in as a volunteer by the local church to head up the counselling work for the child protection team. She offers her time and skills out of a heart of love, to help and support young people and their families." Neil continues to talk as we follow him through the hospital to meet Tandu, who greets us with a bright smile and a firm handshake. She takes over from Neil, showing us into an office and asking about our day.

With her straightened hair and smart jacket, she appears very much the professional, but I can see how the quiet warmth of her personality would encourage the sharing of confidences. She waves aside my appreciation of her precious counselling time, happy to explain how she became involved.

"It all began when a lady who was gang-raped in Malawi had to be sent to Kenya for counselling, as there was no help available in the country. A group of people in Lilongwe decided something needed to be set up locally."

Around this same time, Tandu's church was approached to see if there was anyone already involved in children's ministry who would be interested in helping with the increasing number of cases of child abuse and rape being seen in Blantyre Hospital.

Tandu recollects her enthusiastic response with a smile. "When the church asked me if I would be interested, I said 'Yes!' My heart responded to that need. Perhaps it was because I had a faint memory of child abuse myself when I was very young, by the housekeeper of a neighbour." She looks away as her thoughts go back over the years.

"I remember telling my older sister, 'The guy urinated on me.' I was under five years old because we moved from that area when I was five."

Delighted to be involved in this new project, Tandu joined a group of ten women from across the country to go to South Africa for training, funded by the Network of Organizations for Vulnerable and Orphaned Children (NOVOC). Each woman was encouraged to set up a new project on her return to Malawi, in accordance with her resources and interest. Having already worked with children, Tandu decided to begin with sensitization work in primary schools, tackling the problem at the most vulnerable age.

"Because of our culture we are taught to grow up to respect others, especially elders and adults, but most of the abusers are relatives and people close to the family. A young child really doesn't know what is happening and doesn't even have a name for it. When the adult involved is someone the child knows well, it is easy for a child to think it's normal and allow it to continue for some time."

Tandu realized she needed to alert children to the whole concept of child abuse, explaining that, rather than it being a one-off event, perpetrators would usually groom the child, preparing him or her over a period of time to be receptive to them. It was important for children to know that if someone touched them in a way they didn't like, they should tell someone, an older person who could do something about it. Even if a number of people ignored their story, they should continue telling it until they found someone who believed them.

Tandu explains, "It is very common for children not to be believed, and if the adult response is emphatic enough they may never tell again. I tried to underline the need to talk to the teacher, to the neighbour, to someone."

Having started in schools, Tandu was introduced to the police victim support unit and the work at the hospital. The child protection team was in the process of being set up and she became part of it from the outset, coming to the hospital every Tuesday to counsel children who had been abused. As demand grew, she began to work more days in the week and to train others to work alongside her.

She is grateful for those who are willing to share in the task, realizing she can no longer do it on her own. "We now have a team of ten counsellors who are all volunteers, some with full-time jobs, so it's not always easy to co-ordinate. However, people are enthusiastic and prepared to make the effort to help. As some find they have to leave, we always have others who are ready to join the team."

About six months ago, a young teenager came to the hospital for treatment and was referred to Tandu for counselling. Chiyembekezo has agreed to come and meet me today. It is a token of the relationship of trust that has developed between her and Tandu that she is willing to share such intimate details with a stranger who does not even speak her language.

At this point Chiyembekezo arrives, accompanied by her father. A small fourteen-year-old wearing a striped jumper over a blue dress, she smiles nervously at me as she and her father squeeze into the small room. Neither of them speaks much English and all of us appreciate Tandu being present to ease the situation. Chiyembekezo tucks her feet under the chair and clutches a large handbag on her lap. My usual pre-interview chat, intended to put people at ease, feels somewhat stilted as Tandu translates into Chichewa.

Chiyembekezo agrees that she is happy to share what happened to her so that others can be helped through the services provided at the hospital. In a low voice, hesitant at first, she starts to tell her story, interrupted regularly by the strident ringtone of her father's mobile phone. Sometimes he answers it briefly; sometimes he leaves the room and carries on an energetic conversation on the other side of the door. I try to concentrate on Chiyembekezo.

"My parents divorced when my older sister and I were very young. At first we went with our mother to her village beyond Lilongwe, but when our father came to visit us there, he realized village life was not going to offer the opportunities he wanted for us. He was concerned that we were being neglected and receiving no education, so he brought us back to live with him in an area outside Blantyre. I started school here when I was nine years old."

Five years on, Chiyembekezo was in Standard 5, and much like any other carefree young teenager who enjoyed being with her friends. One evening she and her friends went with great excitement to attend a pre-wedding celebration. Around 200 friends and family had gathered for this important event, and, as was the custom before a wedding, dancing went on throughout the night. In the early hours of the morning, almost at dawn, Chiyembekezo and three of her friends finally left the celebration and headed for home.

Chattering about the events of the evening as they made their way along the path, they were astounded when suddenly a stone seemed to come out of nowhere, striking Chiyembekezo and knocking her to the ground. Looking round, the girls realized they were being followed by a group of about twelve young men, also returning from the celebration. Immediately feeling threatened, and realizing there was no one else around, they started to run. Chiyembekezo, slow to get to her feet, quickly found herself surrounded by the men.

Pleased with their prize, they grabbed her and forced her to walk with them until they came to an empty, half-built house. Stumbling along the path, shaking with fear, Chiyembekezo knew there was no one within earshot. Her friends seemed to have disappeared. As they pushed her ahead of them into the building, dissension arose among the group. Some obviously thought better of what was going on and decided to leave.

As the others left, the remaining group pushed her to the ground. One held his hand over her mouth to silence her screams as three of them raped her, one after the other. When they had finished, she was no longer able to scream. Stunned with shock and pain, she curled up on the ground, uncaring.

Some time later, opening her eyes, she realized that only one of her attackers was still with her. Overcome by some belated concern for her state, he enquired where she lived. When she managed to speak, he helped her to her feet and walked her, distressed and in pain, towards her home. As they came to a bridge near her neighbourhood, he left her to make the rest of the way home alone.

Barely comprehending what had just taken place, Chiyembekezo could only come up with questions. Why had this happened to her? Why had she even gone to the night celebration in the first place? And how would she ever tell her father?

Her father met her at the door, furious that she had stayed out all night. Unable to face his anger, she said nothing but went immediately to bed, exhausted by her ordeal. Somehow she slept, but when she woke she realized she was going to have to tell him. Sore and stiff, she knew he would demand an explanation. Difficult as it was, she stammered her way through the story.

Her father, understandably shocked and angry, took her immediately to the police station near their home. The system ground into gear as the police officer gave them a report to take to the hospital. On arrival, they were directed to an office where they met the social welfare officer and filled in the details of the story. A pleasant lady doctor examined Chiyembekezo, did some tests, and gave her medication. Grateful to have people around her who seemed to know what to do, Chiyembekezo submitted to all that was needed. A social worker reassured her that the team in the hospital would continue to care for her and work with the police to investigate what had happened.

"We would like you to come back to the hospital on Tuesday to see a counsellor," said the social worker. "She will help you cope with what has happened to you. You will also need some injections and ongoing medication. You can go home now but we will be following up your story through the team here."

On the Tuesday, Chiyembekezo came to the hospital again with her father, as requested, and was shown to the counselling room, where she met Tandu. Although Tandu was pleasant and reassuring, Chiyembekezo found it hard to talk to anyone about her experience. Unable to put into words what had happened, she sat with her eyes on the floor, leaving her father to relate the story as far as he knew it. Tandu encouraged her to come back again the following Tuesday and gradually, week by week, Chiyembekezo began to respond. As she came to know and trust Tandu, she was able to be more open about her feelings. Tandu seemed to understand and was able to listen without blaming her for what had happened.

Once the initial shock of the experience had worn off, the question confronting the fourteen-year-old was the risk of HIV. She was pleased when she tested negative, but had to come for further tests after three months, as the initial test is not always conclusive. During those three months, the thought of HIV was never far from her mind. It was a great relief when the second test also proved negative; she realized a different outcome could have had far-reaching implications for her life.

Meanwhile, the police were following up the case. A friend who escaped on the night of the rape recognized one of the men and was able to identify him to the police. Although he was brought in for questioning, he was released after a few days. The men lived locally and were known in the neighbourhood; they reacted fiercely when their friend was arrested, threatening the girls and their families. Chiyembekezo felt very vulnerable; her sister was at boarding school and her father was busy with his onion business during the day. Struggling to make enough money to support the family, he also worked as a security guard at night, leaving her alone at home for much of the time. Concerned for her safety, he sent her to stay with a relative in another town while he organized a permanent move for the family.

Trying to do his best in the situation, Chiyembekezo's father felt out of his depth, struggling in his mind with a number of concerns. Now that she had experienced sex with men, he was worried that his daughter would become promiscuous. On one occasion, after they had moved house, she wanted to return to visit her cousin in the area where they used to live. When her father refused to give permission, she ended up going anyway, leaving him worried and anxious.

Sitting at home, his thoughts ranged over the situation, jumping from one possibility to another. "Surely, after what has happened, she would never want to revisit that place. Why is she so keen to go there? What is going on in her life?"

When she eventually returned, his fear for her overflowed into anger and he ended up beating her. Afterwards, guilty about his reaction and conscious that he didn't know how to handle the situation, he realized he needed someone to listen to his concerns and help him deal with them. He turned to Tandu, confiding in her his fears for his daughter's well-being.

Tandu explained that sexual promiscuity was only likely to result if a girl was left without any feeling of self-worth. If she realized the rape was not her choice and she had nothing to feel guilty about, it would bolster her emotional well-being and help her think positively about herself.

"Just be there for her," Tandu told him. "Help her feel special as a person and support her. That will help her not to go down the promiscuity route."

With limited experience of family life himself, Chiyembekezo's father found it difficult to understand the issues facing a teenage girl. Having grown up as an orphan, living with distant relatives, all he wanted when he grew up was to have children of his own and be able to give them the kind of love he had not received from his own parents. He would have liked a son, but when he had only two girls he accepted what God had given and vowed to do his best for them. From the little he had, he had tried to provide for them and their needs, but now felt he was a failure because of what had happened and guilty that he had not been there.

Tandu encouraged him. "The girls see your efforts and all that you do for them, even getting an extra job to pay for your first daughter's secondary-school fees. I'm sure it is something that they appreciate. It shows how much you feel for them and want to see them succeed. Tell them how you feel and it will help them."

This was a revelation to a father who, in that culture, would never normally have such a conversation with his daughters. Yet Tandu was obviously trained and experienced and knew what she was talking about. He listened to her advice and followed it as best he could.

Chiyembekezo has become more comfortable as the discussion has continued, and more articulate about her feelings. She looks me in the eye as she explains, "Six months have passed since that event. I am happier now because I used to think all the time about what happened to me, but now it comes less to my mind. Tandu helped me, especially with encouraging me to continue working hard at school, and I'm doing well now. I complete Standard 5 next month and I want to keep on and finish primary school.

"The experience has changed how I feel about men because I realize I need to be careful – I can't go out at night. Since they raped me, I see men as nothing. I didn't like what they did to me and I know they can always do that to me again if they get the opportunity. Fear still comes when the memory comes back and I remember the terror of that night."

These days, if there is no one at home, Chiyembekezo

goes to stay overnight with a nearby relative, where she enjoys the company of the young people in the home. Her sister has returned from boarding school as her father could no longer afford the fees, so she now attends secondary school locally and the girls are company for each other. The family attends church and Chiyembekezo tells me that she finds comfort in prayer.

"I pray in the afternoons when there is no one there at my relative's house. I find it very hard to be alone at home but it helps when I talk to God about it."

Chiyembekezo is concerned that justice has not been done and the men have never been punished for raping her. As a counsellor, Tandu's role is to support clients, helping them deal with the trauma, and she encourages social workers to follow up the justice side. However, lack of sufficient personnel often means that cases are not pursued.

Deciding to follow up this case personally, Tandu went to the police station to meet the investigating officer, armed with the identity of the man known by the girls and information on his whereabouts. Presenting the file, she told him, "You have one of them and there are three other guys to be dealt with also."

He replied, "I was waiting for the father to come so we can go to their houses."

When Chiyembekezo's father went to the police station he was told, "Don't worry, you don't need to go to court with her; we will let you know the outcome."

The only outcome to be seen, however, is that the man is now back in the neighbourhood. When the family moved out of the area, Chiyembekezo's father could not take time off work to continue to follow it up any further and there is a limit to what Tandu can do. It was referred to the Department of Public Prosecution, who provide government lawyers to look into cases where there are problems.

Tandu says, "When I am working with a client, I know they are concerned about what is happening legally and I know there is no way I can get through to them if they have those worries. So usually I work with the police and keep on following up what is happening. Working with the Department of Public Prosecution, we can meet here in the hospital and look at the case and I know they will follow it up.

"Sometimes it is just too much effort for the family to follow up the case. We might have to go to the court seven times, and most of the families don't have time because of work. Even to have one day off is difficult, so they just get tired and give up. Evidence is difficult too. Nowadays we are beginning to get children coming in more quickly after it happens, but often it is a few days later by the time children start to talk or the mother finds blood on the underwear. By the time they come here it is not always easy for doctors to find evidence to satisfy the court. They really have to have proof of penetration for someone to be charged with rape. Unless there is another witness it is difficult to get a conviction."

Tandu underlines that Chiyembekezo's case is one of the comparatively few abuse cases involving a stranger. Ninety-five per cent of abuse is carried out by family members and relatives, and often the family don't want to go ahead with prosecution when the perpetrator is a relative; sometimes they just run out of patience with the system.

Tandu realizes they continue to face many challenges as they seek to re-educate people about abuse. "When a young child speaks up about abuse the parents often beat her, because they think it is the child's fault. They will ask, 'Why were you there?' The parents just don't know what to do. We try to explain to parents that what the child needs is support rather than recrimination, and we encourage them to make use of the child protection network."

The team see thirty cases a month now in the Queen Elizabeth Hospital. It is obvious there should be many more prosecutions than there are. Tandu is realistic about it.

"Sometimes the family will agree to go to the police if they can see it as something other than a personal issue between them and their relative. We tell them, 'It is not you who are prosecuting; it is the police.' However, we can't force the family to keep pushing the case if the police do not carry it through. There are many frustrations in this work and I think, 'Am I going to be able to help them through the whole justice system or should I just help them deal with what has happened, the trauma and resulting situations in their lives?' Some stories are so complicated, and we already know how the system works. We just have to try to concentrate on helping where we can."

Sometimes a girl is so distressed she is unable to speak about it, ending up in tears every time she tries to share what happened. Tandu will keep seeing her until she feels safe enough to talk. With the very young cases, counsellors work mostly with the mother, but they also do developmental touch-and-play therapy with young children. They teach the mother games she can use at home with the child, depending on the problem – some children have already changed in their behaviour by the time they come to the hospital and are afraid of men, unable to go anywhere near a man without getting upset. The team encourage the mother to see that it's a matter of being with her child and showing her appropriate touch so she can gradually feel comfortable again.

Tandu smiles as she underlines her reason for persisting in her role despite its frustrations. "I feel God has called me into this particular work. It is encouraging because it is something new in Malawi. We try to get people to understand what we are attempting to do. The concept of counselling is often understood here as advice, but that's not what we are doing – it's about them having someone to talk to and finding their own way through. We are just providing someone who will hold their hand through the process. We want to reach out and bring God's love into a painful situation."

We say goodbye to Chiyembekezo and her father and leave Tandu to pick up her next appointment. I carry the image of Chiyembekezo's shy smile with me as we part. Our short experience here in Blantyre has shown us a powerful example of the church operating as salt and light in the community – Christian students and doctors active in the government hospital, the local church working alongside the hospital and other statutory bodies, Christians working out their faith in the marketplace.

7
Sarah

"Just put the fingers of your right hand on the screen, please, madam. Now the left."

The last time I did this was in America. The modern security device takes me by surprise as we process smoothly through immigration at Nairobi Airport. Collecting our luggage in the arrivals hall, we are met by Thomas Leremore, a tall smiling Samburu who shepherds us out of the airport to his Land Cruiser, in which he whisks us efficiently through the turmoil of Nairobi traffic. The number of vehicles on the road seems to have multiplied exponentially since we were last here six years ago, and the prospect of confronting this maelstrom without a local expert at the wheel fills me with dismay.

As he drives, Thomas talks about his studies. Trying to complete a Master's degree in Peace and Reconciliation, he is frustrated by the inaccessibility of his tutor, but while he waits for the process to work itself out he carries on various consultancy and business ventures. Delivering us safely to our destination, he and his Irish wife Naomi welcome us to their comfortable home in one of the many gated compounds in the city, security maintained by an electric fence and a twenty-four-hour guard. Their two engaging young sons tug at our hearts, reminding us of our two lively little grandsons in Scotland.

Thomas's mother, living at the opposite extreme, both geographically and culturally, from her rural home hundreds of kilometres north, seems to have adjusted to life in the city, caring for her grandchildren in the age-old pattern of African life.

Thomas comments, "She doesn't like the city but she likes being with her grandchildren." We resurrect our rusty Swahili to respond to this tiny lady's bright smile and firm handshake. Another son, Joseph, a councillor in Maralal in the north, is also living in the house while extending his studies in Nairobi in preparation for next year's elections, and she seems content to have her family around her.

Next morning we rise early. It is six years since our last visit to Kenya and we are eager to see what the day will bring.

"Right, kids. Time for nursery. We're leaving." Naomi rounds up her two reluctant toddlers and shepherds them towards the vehicle.

"I'm taking Jean and Brian to visit Sarah at the orphanage today and we need to get on the road. Into the car, everyone." With cheerful determination Naomi sweeps children and guests into the vehicle, waves her thanks to the guard on the gate, and we take our place in the crawling Nairobi rush hour. The roundabout sits like a giant octopus, its tentacles drawing in a multitude of assorted vehicles. When ours will be absorbed is anybody's guess.

We eventually drop the children at nursery and head

out of Nairobi on the Thika road, which is in the process of being expanded to an eight-lane superhighway at a cost of 31 billion Kenyan shillings (KES), around £220 million. Part of a direct corridor up through Africa to the Sudan, which is being constructed by the Chinese, it will be an amazing asset when completed, but just now presents a conglomeration of half-built roads, unfinished surfaces, bumps and gulleys that combine to confuse the unwary driver. Vehicles packed with passengers approach us from all sides. It is a matter of conjecture where the actual road is supposed to be. A lorry lies on its side where it has fallen off the edge, its load strewn over the surrounding highway, small figures buzzing around the catastrophe. Naomi holds to the road with ruthless determination and, undeterred, delivers us to Joy Children's Home in Ruiru, shaken but grateful to have got there in one piece.

Sarah Wanjiku welcomes us into her office, offering tea and a plentiful supply of bananas. Her infectious laugh and cheerful approach to life indicate that Joy Children's Home is well named. As the others leave for a tour of the compound, I ask her how the home came to be.

"I was one of thirteen children," Sarah explains, finishing her tea, "so I had no shortage of childminders. As a young child, I suffered from recurring malaria and the high fever would sometimes cause me to fit. One evening when I became unwell, my mother took me as usual to the local government hospital, only to find they were short of drugs. The following morning she left me in my sister's care while she returned as requested to collect the medicine."

Normally, the household cooking was done over an open fire outside, but because of the cold July weather a fire had been lit in the kitchen that morning. Sarah's father was asleep nearby and her sister was preparing breakfast over a stove in another room when two-year-old Sarah had a fit and fell into the fire. With the porridge ready, Sarah's sister came looking for her. Hearing a groaning noise, she looked around, saw her in the fire, and yelled in horror, waking her father. People came running to grab the toddler and take her outside, trying to pull off the burning nylon clothes which were now stuck to her body. Looking at me across her desk, Sarah shakes her head as she comments, "I was only two years old but I can still remember that pain."

Sarah remained in intensive care in Kenyatta Hospital in Nairobi while they fought to save her life. Her severely burned left arm had to be removed above the elbow. As the other burns began to heal, she discovered she was doubled over, with tissue from her stomach and leg fused together. An operation to separate them left her with a deep scar on her stomach but she was grateful to be able to straighten again. Her father sold a piece of land to pay for her hospital costs.

Back at home, life had changed. Suddenly she was a disabled child, with no prospect of ever accomplishing anything. Reluctant to send this disabled child to school, unable to see how she could benefit from education, the family saw Sarah's role as being the one who would stay at home and take care of all that was needed there. As she grew old enough to understand, Sarah rebelled against this sentence, crying to be allowed to go to school like other children. Her family finally relented, but her attendance was intermittent; at the onset of any domestic crisis, she was the first to be called on to take care of children and home.

At school, however, Sarah had come to the attention of one of the teachers who, concerned about her frequent absences, visited the family, trying unsuccessfully to reason with Sarah's mother.

One day an American Jewish couple visited the school, with the specific wish to support a disabled child from a poor family. Touched by Sarah's story, they went to visit the family home. Unable to speak English, Sarah and her mother listened as the teacher interpreted the strangers' amazing words – they wanted to take care of her and pay for her to go to school. With her mother's agreement, Sarah returned to school, astonished that someone was so interested in her despite her disability.

Although she now had the assurance of sponsorship, problems persisted for the young Sarah. Sometimes the promised money did not reach the school, despite being sent faithfully to the partner organization, and Sarah was sent home from school because of unpaid fees or lack of shoes or uniform. Despite this she persisted, studying as hard as she could, borrowing books from classmates, and negotiating an extra hour with teachers when possible in an attempt to make up for time when she was barred from school. When she was in Standard 7, her sponsors came again to visit her. Looking at her school reports, they were taken aback by her disappointing results. With her improved English, she tried to explain the situation.

"Sometimes I am sent home because my fees have not been paid; sometimes I have to borrow textbooks from my friends; sometimes I have no uniform."

Disturbed that the money they sent was not being processed in any regular fashion, her sponsors took Sarah out shopping. Together they bought all the books, clothes, and shoes she needed. For Sarah it was like Christmas, and yet it was beyond any Christmas she had ever experienced. Chattering with excitement she returned home, accompanied by the visitors laden with all her purchases.

Her mother, however, was unimpressed by all this spending on Sarah. Turning to her daughter, who was now able to translate for her, she asked her to interpret her words to the sponsors.

"Don't waste your money on this girl. If you could buy a large water tank for our family, that would be more useful. I would be able to do some farming and support *all* my children, not just this one."

Angry at her mother and terrified that the sponsors would agree, Sarah was in tears as she was forced to pass on her mother's appeal. The wonderful day was ruined. Her dream of education might be at an end after all. The understanding sponsors, however, were not swayed by her mother's feelings. As they left, they reassured her.

"Sarah, we will not stop supporting you. We will not do what your mother is asking; we will do what our hearts are telling us. We want you to be a responsible, independent person in the future. We will speak to the partner organization and sort out the money situation. Don't worry about anything; just concentrate on your studies, and we will look after everything else."

Sarah returned to school, redoubling her efforts,

determined to make her sponsors proud of her. Doing well in her Standard 8 exams, she was admitted to a good secondary boarding school. When she reached Form 2, however, the problem of unpaid fees arose again. Embarrassed, she found her way to the office of the organization handling the money and approached the administrator.

"Kathleen, can't you pay my fees?"

"I'm sorry, Sarah, we don't have the money."

"Then give me a contact number for my sponsors so I can talk to them directly. Do you mean I will not be able to continue my secondary-school education?"

"You need to ask your mother those questions. She is the one who bore you. She is the one responsible for you."

Upset by this bitter exchange, Sarah went to her head teacher in despair.

"I am taking my bag and going home. When God gives me another chance I will come back. I cannot concentrate with all the problems about school fees."

Returning home, Sarah turned to God in desperation. Near where she lived was a small forest where the young teenager began to retreat to pray and fast, praying that God would do something. When she was not there, she spent her time helping her mother in the home and on the farm.

One day a child arrived with an envelope from her headmaster. Opening it, Sarah was appalled to read a letter from her main sponsor saying he was glad to hear how well she was progressing at school and of the support she was receiving from the aid organization. He was oblivious to her true situation.

On the outside of the envelope, the sponsor had written his address. Borrowing twenty shillings from her father for postage, Sarah replied to the letter, explaining her circumstances. Two weeks later, the sponsor telephoned the headmaster directly. On his instructions, the headmaster came personally to collect Sarah, bringing her back to school to continue her studies. Disassociating himself from the aid organization, the sponsor sent the money directly to the school so that she was able to complete her education without further financial concerns. After school, he continued to support her in college while she studied computing, then trained as a primary-school teacher, specializing in early childhood studies.

Smiling, she says, "The person who really encouraged me was my sponsor. All the knowledge I have came through him. When I went on the computer course, a computer was very expensive. There was no way I could have done that without him. He continued to visit me in Kenya; he really empowered me."

As Sarah reflected on her experience with this stranger who had become a friend, a desire was growing in her heart. One day she expressed her dream to her mother.

"I am studying now, but when I have my first salary I will take an orphan, a needy child whom I don't know, who is not my relative, and help her. I will send her to school. Don't depend on my first salary, because I am going to use it for that purpose."

Needless to say, her mother was not impressed by this idea. She called on other members of the family to talk to her, but Sarah was adamant.

"Someone I didn't know has taken care of me, someone not from my tribe, not even my colour; they just came and took me to school. I have to do that for somebody else. If it had not been for God, I would not have made it in life; I would not have survived school. I have to give something back."

Unable to make any headway, the relatives reported back to her mother, "She is just talking like that because she is young. Leave her. When she starts working she will be different; she will support you."

Immediately after college, Sarah got a job as a government teacher and was posted to Mathare slum in Nairobi, where she discovered problems she had never encountered before.

"I found so many needy children and orphans. Not only had their parents died, but they had no house to live in. I realized I had been lucky to have parents, home, and food. I was amazed to see orphans, even under three years old, being used by people to sell drugs and traditional beer. Those children had no parents, no relatives. In college I had learned the theory of how we can mould a child under six years of age but now I was seeing those children being abused and spoiled while they were still so young. I felt for them. I could see that, as they grew older and had children themselves, the problems would continue. Who would care for their children? That cycle of poverty and need would never be broken while their circumstances remained unchanged. Typically what happens is that a young mother becomes a prostitute because her own parents have died and she has to do what she can to get food. Men make use of her and infect her with HIV, which she passes on to her children. Then she dies and leaves the next generation of children struggling as orphans, and so the cycle continues."

Sarah had not been in Mathare very long before she saw this scenario being played out in her class at school. When one young boy stopped attending, she assumed he had moved from the city, perhaps having been taken to his family home in a rural area. On making enquiries, however, she discovered he had stopped coming because his parents had died. Seeing the opportunity to put her long-held dream into action, she told him to come to school and she would pay his fees. At lunch time she sat with him and shared her lunch with the hungry child.

Winnie was a very bright girl in Sarah's class to whom she became very attached. When she suddenly disappeared from class, Sarah assumed regretfully that she had gone back home to western Kenya. After a few months, however, Sarah met the six-year-old one day, unkempt and dirty, carrying a baby.

Sarah, surprised to see her, said, "Winnie, I have missed you in school. Where have you been?"

Hanging her head, the child replied, "I have been here."

"What happened? Why are you not coming to school?"

"My mother died."

"Because your mother died, you don't come to school? What are you doing now?"

"I am taking care of this baby for another woman, and she gives me food."

Taking Winnie by the hand, Sarah went to the home of the woman concerned. Although the mother was not to be found, Sarah discovered that the six-year-old was actually caring for three small children. Returning to school, she shared the story with her colleagues.

"This is dreadful. What can I do?"

They spoke as those who had heard this story many times. "You will make yourself ill. You can't help everyone in Mathare."

"But even if we can't help everybody, can't we help two or three and feel we have done something in life?"

"You don't have any children of your own yet. When you have your own children, you won't be able to do that."

"But can't we contribute something, do *something*, to allow that girl to attend school?" There was no answer. The problem was too immense for them to envisage a solution.

Refusing to be discouraged, Sarah went to the head teacher of her school.

"There is something I want you to help me do. I want to care for Winnie. If I can take her from that home, I can bring her to school."

"And where will she live?"

"Can we not find someone who would be caring, who would allow her to live with them and attend school?"

Unable to find such a family, Sarah began visiting Winnie and taking her food. Soon, however, she realized she was feeding not just Winnie but the whole family, as there was no way the child was eating all that Sarah was providing. Taking advantage of Sarah's concern for the child, the family were taking all that she was willing to offer.

Frustrated and not knowing the way forward, Sarah wrote to her sponsor, sharing her story. She was not looking for any particular reaction, but felt he was someone who would understand her feelings.

She wrote, "It is so hard to be a teacher in the slum. Should I change my occupation, or what should I do? I can't stay here seeing all these things happening to the children. I feel so helpless."

The response of his kind heart was immediate. "Sarah, you are doing very important work supporting those children. How many are you trying to care for now? Can we pay the school fees for them? What is the best way for us to help you?"

Sarah did not have to think for long. "There are a number of things we need to do. The first is to get them a house, and somebody to take care of them. Then after that we need to provide food and school fees. We can't do one of these without the other because if they have no food they will still drop out of school. A hungry child cannot go to school. A lot of children are not achieving their potential because they don't have the basics of food and shelter."

Sarah's desire was to move them from the slum into a different environment. With her sponsor's backing she found a house in Ruiru, about twenty-four kilometres from Nairobi. Her desire was to use the money wisely, buying not just the essentials but also clothes that would look smart on the children. By the time they moved to the house, she had ten children, aged three and four years old, with one room for the boys, one for the girls, and one for a library so that she could encourage them to read.

Just as Sarah was settling in with her children, she received a telephone call from the government department with responsibility for children.

"Are you Sarah Wanjiku, who is setting up the children's home in Ruiru? Please come and see me at the children's department in Thika."

Sarah was taken aback. "It's not a home, it's just my house."

"Are those children yours?"

"No, but their parents died and I am caring for them."

"Then you need to come and see us at Thika."

Sarah did not go. Trying to ignore the matter, she hoped they would forget about her, but eventually she received a call saying that if she did not come, they would come for her. Apprehensive, not knowing what lay ahead, she went to Thika. She was only twenty-five years old and had no experience of dealing with government departments. In the office she tried to explain her position.

"I did not mean to do anything wrong; I did not have any bad intention. I just want to care for those children."

Their response was kinder than she expected. "You are doing very good work but you have to be registered to set up a children's home."

She said, "I don't want to run a children's home. I just want to care for those children. I know of another case where a woman in Nairobi had a home and she ended up with too many children in the orphanage and couldn't manage the stress. The children were suffering; the woman was suffering. So I don't want a children's home. I would not be able to manage a children's home. I just want to look after these children in my own home."

"I'm sorry; if you want to look after these children, you have to register. We will help you with everything. What is the name of your home going to be?"

The answer was easy. "It will be called Joy Children's Home." Those children were not happy in the slum; Sarah wanted them to have a little joy in their new home.

They sent her a certificate and Joy Children's Home became official. All of a sudden, with registration, the scenario she had dreaded became a reality: the government began to refer children for whom they needed help. Within a few weeks, Sarah found herself with sixteen children and very little food. When she tried to explain that she couldn't take any more, they replied that there was nowhere else to send them.

Then, within a year of setting up her home, Sarah received an email informing her of the sudden death of her sponsor from a brain tumour. In a moment she realized she had lost not just her main source of income, but a true friend and confidant. Before she had time to recover from the shock, the people he worked with contacted her with an astounding message.

"If you want us to continue supporting the orphanage, you have to stop teaching children about Christianity in that home." In disbelief, Sarah explained that she could not stop talking about Jesus to the children. His love was the reason she had set it up in the first place. They withdrew the sponsorship.

Sarah was left with sixteen children between the ages of eighteen months and five years. Almost all the workers in the orphanage withdrew after the first month, when they realized there was no salary. She didn't know where to turn or what to do.

One person remained faithful to her, however. Mike was a social worker who had been part of the home from the outset. An orphan himself, he had been brought up by his grandparents.

When everyone else left he said to Sarah, "I have qualifications, I can get work elsewhere, but I cannot leave these children. I know how I suffered when my mother died and I cannot abandon them to go and work somewhere else."

He looked at Sarah, now crying continuously as she thought of the high rent which she could not even begin to pay.

"We will be thrown out of this house." She was inconsolable.

Mike had seen God at work in the past. "Have faith, Sarah. We will survive."

Each week the children attended Sunday school at the local church. At this stage, Naomi, our hostess, was coming each Wednesday to work with the Sunday-school teachers. Seeing the children in their pretty pink and grey uniforms, Naomi came to visit Joy Children's Home and struck up an instant rapport with Sarah. Before long she realized the financial pressure under which Sarah was living, and decided to do what she could to help.

Sarah reminisces, "I remember how Naomi came to see me and encourage me. Every Wednesday, for almost six months, she gave me 1,000 Kenyan shillings. Every week

I would pray that she would come again that Wednesday. She did not know how happy I was that I could buy food for the kids, and somehow it was enough that we could have vegetables and fruit for a week. We continued like that. Others helped, and somehow we always just managed to survive."

Gradually a network of support grew as people became aware of her situation. Sarah had saved some money while she was teaching. She decided to try to construct a building of her own, so that she would not have the constant worry of finding rent. She talked to a lady selling a plot of land for 400,000 Kenyan shillings, explaining that she had only 150,000.

Her reply amazed Sarah. "Give me the money you have, start building, and then when you get more children in the orphanage you will have money and you can pay me the rest later." Taking her at her word, Sarah started building. Before she had finished, however, the lady was overwhelmed by Sarah's concern for the little ones.

"Just take care of the children," she said. "Don't think about the money. I am making a donation; I know what you are going through and the good work you are doing. I want you to be able to carry on without worrying about money."

Seeing God's hand in the situation, Sarah was filled with gratitude for all he had done for her.

Concerned for the future of the children, she registered the building in the name of Joy Children's Home. "Even if I am not here, no one can ask the children to leave, because the building is in their name. Some of my relatives thought I was not taking care of my own family and there was some ill feeling against me because of that, so it seemed wiser not to have the building in my own name. If anything happens to me, no one can take this place or grab their things. Everything belongs to the children and they are protected."

Sarah tried to keep the children looking good, despite their straitened circumstances.

One person said to her, "You are keeping those children very smart – no one will support you. They look too well cared for."

Sarah was disgusted. "I thought, 'I cannot keep the children dirty just so that people come and support me. I am going to do everything well for them. God will give us the people who will support us.'"

The same principle applied to the building. People advised her to use corrugated iron to save money, but she was determined to build a stone house. Approaching a quarry owner, she asked if she could borrow stones, as she did not have the money to buy. It led to an interesting exchange.

"I don't have money, but children are suffering. Can you help me, even if it's a lorry load of stones?"

She knew it was unheard of for someone to give a lorry load of stones. But she kept singing the song "When there is no way, God can make a way". She knew that even when there seemed to be no way forward, God could bring it about.

The owner looked at her in disbelief. "You are talking about building a stone house and you have no money. Are you mad?"

"I am sorry; I am not mad but I have children who are suffering, so I have to do something. I was employed as a teacher but I resigned to care for these children. Where can I get money? That is why I am coming to you. Let me tell you, I hate borrowing; I hate having children without being stable in life, but this is what I have come through, so please can you help me for the sake of those children?"

The man relented and gave her a lorry load of stones; another gave her two loads and gradually she gathered together the necessary building materials. As building commenced, people looked on in amazement, wondering how she had managed to do it.

Sarah knows that God has his hand on it all. "The church in the UK has really helped us. Sometimes it seems like a huge miracle. Sometimes at Christmas we get a large gift. That's how this building has been completed. At times we don't have enough food; it can be stressful, but we thank God the children are very healthy and very bright. Sometimes we are supported with porridge, from the African Child Fund, so we can feed the children. Despite the challenges, we always get through. We don't have a permanent sponsor but many different people help – some with small amounts and some with large amounts. We never know where it is going to come from. We are praying that one day God will provide a permanent sponsor.

"In the meantime, trusting in God from day to day keeps our faith alive and we never become hungry. Since January we have been getting fruit: today we have lots of bananas; tomorrow something different will come. We don't know how God works; we just know he does and we thank him for that. Perhaps he doesn't want us to be proud; we have to depend on him so that we give him the glory. God knows what we need and how we survive. When the helpers come and tell me we are short of food, I just say, 'Tell the children to pray.'"

When Sarah built the home, it was seven kilometres from the nearest government school, too far for the children to walk. She made one of the rooms into a classroom, divided the children into age groups, and taught them herself. When other needy children from the community around wanted to join her class, she was unable to refuse but realized the numbers were quickly getting too large for her to cope with, and she had no money to pay teachers. When teachers approached her looking for a job, she explained that in the home they were surviving by faith; they had no regular source of money.

She says, "Some cannot live that way, but some caught the vision and were willing to come and teach."

With the addition of teachers the numbers of children coming to school spiralled, but the pragmatic Sarah was undaunted.

"Some parents were not poor so we asked them to give something to show appreciation for the teachers, even if it was not a salary. That's how we are surviving now. Those parents who are able to, contribute what they can. About seventy-five children in our school cannot give anything; if we charged fees, they would have to leave. We have good teachers and we thank God for all that he has done in bringing them to us. Now we want to separate home and school because we have 200 pupils altogether. We have twenty-four children in the orphanage, seventy-five needy children from the local community who attend the school, and the others who contribute what they can. But the place is too small for so many children, so we have to build again."

A Norwegian church has now helped to buy another plot of land beside the existing orphanage, where a new home is planned for the children. There are plans to have cows and a biogas system, and large separate dormitories for boys and girls. The existing site will become a primary school, complete with classrooms, library, and sewing room.

In 2008, Sarah's life took an exciting new turn when she met a young man, Jimnah, on a course she was attending in Nairobi. A previous relationship had foundered when the man concerned refused to accept the children as an essential part of Sarah's life, leaving her sceptical of men. Jimnah, however, was persistent, and one year later, in April 2009, they became husband and wife, with all the children as attendants at the wedding. Because of her deep scarring from the fire, the doctors had serious concerns when Sarah became pregnant, but despite all predictions she managed to have a healthy baby girl, understandably named Precious Joy.

Sarah is constantly grateful for all God has done.

"'With God all things are possible,'" she says, a smile lighting up her face. "I have it written up here on the wall in the home to remind us of that truth. That's what I believe; there are no hard things with God."

8

Kasoni

I lean forward in my seat with an anxious eye on competing vehicles as we make our first independent venture onto the Nairobi roads. Our route through the suburbs takes us past areas familiar to us, but we are amazed at the changes since our last visit. Large detached houses with spacious gardens have been replaced by townhouse and apartment complexes. Leafy avenues have been taken over by office-block developments. The relentless influx of people to the capital is reflected in the concentration of new building surrounded by a constant swirl of traffic.

We turn from the melee of vehicles around us into the oasis of the Mennonite Guest House. In the lobby I meet Kasoni, a beautiful Samburu girl who greets us with warmth and poise, less perturbed than we are by the morning journey through the city. Forced inside by the chilly June day, I abandon my hope of sitting in the garden and we find a quiet corner in the dining room where we can talk without fear of interruption.

The girl's screams seemed to cut through the heart of six-year-old Kasoni. She and her friends had been invited to go and watch the circumcision ritual, so that when their time came they would be prepared for what was going to happen. They had not yet started school; they knew only the *manyattas*[1] of their home area. Aware that circumcision was a very important part of life in their family and tribe, and thinking it would be exciting and fun, the young girls had gone happily with others to the home where the teenager was to be circumcised.

As she watched the circumciser cut into the girl's flesh and completely remove all her external genitalia, Kasoni was terrified by the amount of blood that seemed to be everywhere. The girl being circumcised sagged in the arms of those who held her and lost consciousness as the circumciser completed her task. They left her to bleed for a time before starting to pour milk and water over the wound.

Kasoni knew there was something wrong. This could not be the circumcision rite that everyone talked about so excitedly. Fighting her way through the spectators, she ran all the way home to the familiar comfort of her mother, blurting out the story of what she had just witnessed.

"Is that what you say is circumcision?"

"Yes."

"OK, then, if that is it, I will not do it." She was still shaking from the ordeal.

Her mother laughed gently. She knew her small child would grow up to understand the necessity of the cut.

Kasoni was never lonely as a child. With four brothers and four sisters in her immediate family, and her mother the first of her father's three wives, she was always surrounded by people. The mud walls of her home provided shelter at night but most of life was lived outdoors, in the company of the extended family. Living in South Horr, almost 400 kilometres north of Nairobi, she grew up in an area with a strong Samburu culture, from which she drew her identity and stability.

At six years old Kasoni started nursery school, and progressed into Standard 1 of primary school two years later, accepting the forty-five minute walk as part of the school day. In the school holidays she and her siblings, like all Samburu children, looked after the family's animals. Their father was a wealthy farmer of goats, camels, and cows, and before long he decided that all the children should stay at home to look after his large herd. Determined to go to school and learn, despite not quite understanding the full significance of education, Kasoni objected to this demand. Reluctantly, her father agreed to her staying in school, provided that she continue to join her two younger siblings in looking after the animals during the holidays.

When she was eleven years old, Kasoni moved from her own village during term time to stay with her cousin, who lived closer to the school. Throughout the following years her cousin supported her in her desire for education. Fees were not a problem as primary education was free, the only cost being the fee to sit the KCPE (Kenya Certificate of Primary Education) final examination. Kasoni began to think about attending church. She had no real desire to follow God, but knew that church was a good place to find a sponsor for secondary-school fees. God, however, had other plans for her life.

Around this time she heard about Stephen and Angelina, Irish missionaries in the nearby town of Tuum, who held regular youth camps for children and young people in the school holidays. As Kasoni began to attend these, she heard a variety of speakers, from both Kenya and elsewhere.

At first, she had very little understanding of the message that was being presented. She had no concept of Jesus and the Holy Spirit. Traditionally, Samburu people knew that there was a God, and her parents had brought the family up in the Catholic Church, but in practice they had a mixture of beliefs.

She explains, "We believe God is in Mount Nyiru, and the Samburu have always offered animal sacrifices there on the mountain. My family used to go to church but they also held on to their traditional beliefs. Although they paid lip service to modern forms of religion in the shape of Christianity, the traditional beliefs were very deep and they did not want to turn their back on them."

Although Kasoni was attending a Catholic primary school, her focus was purely on study and school work; the church as such held no interest for her. Then in Standard 6, at the age of thirteen, her life changed at one of the youth camps in South Horr. For the first time she realized that Jesus was real and alive, and, confronted with the challenge to follow him, she knew she had to respond. As she committed her life to him, she was aware that everything had changed.

Kasoni's face lights up as she looks back on the event that turned her life around. "I used to go to church simply as a routine, but the power I received at that time led to a transformation in my life. The Holy Spirit came in and opened up my mind to understand who God is and how Jesus and the Holy Spirit could work within me. My father was very opposed to my open decision to follow Christ. In Samburu culture women have no say; they follow the decisions the men make, so my father did not like me making a decision like this independently and my mother had to agree with my father."

Kasoni marked her decision by giving herself the name "Faith". Almost immediately she became aware of elements of her traditional culture that flew in the face of her new way of life. The most pressing issue was the all-important ritual of female circumcision. She stares past me into the middle distance as she reflects on it.

"Female circumcision is a must if you are to be recognized as a person in the community, so everyone must undergo it. You are taken to another level when you become a 'proper' woman. There are other rituals involving the sacrifice of sheep and goats which take place when you are a teenager, before the ritual, before you undergo the cut. The family prepare everything, they buy big bags of sugar, they slaughter goats and even cows, and all the Samburu celebrate together. The sheep and the goats are significant. Even if the family has never slaughtered these animals before, even when their daughter was born, they have to do it when she becomes a woman. The girl wears a special skin prepared for the event and, even though she is big, she is held like a baby. They pronounce words over her life that are not godly."

One day, shortly after Kasoni's decision to follow Christ, she was helping her mother prepare food for the family. She handed her mother the packet of maize meal and knelt down to encourage the sticks in the fire to a brighter flame. The younger ones would be back soon with the goats and her father from his meeting in the village. The sun was sinking behind the distant hills, leaving them silhouetted like a row of camels against the pink-tinged sky. The coolness of the day made her duties easier.

The older woman poured maize meal and water into the blackened pot, red earth from the ground darkening the edge of the cloth she wore around her waist.

"Your father has been talking to me, my daughter. He has prepared everything. You will soon be a real woman at last."

Kasoni kept her eyes on the fire. "I am not ready. I want to finish this year at school." She crouched over the reddening fire.

"School will not be of any benefit when you are married. You bring shame on the whole family by refusing to obey your father and ignoring the traditions of our tribe."

Her mother thumped the pot down on the fire, brushing Kasoni aside. "How many other girls your age do you know who have not received the cut? Do you want to be mocked wherever you go?"

Kasoni hung her head, her eyes filling with tears. This was so hard. The aroma of cooking maize meal, the wooden spoon thudding against the pot, her mother's comforting presence – these things had been her life from the day she was born. Could she really turn her back on her culture?

"Of course I don't want to be mocked. I value the traditions of our elders. But I value education also. Please let me wait a bit longer. I am still young. Just give me one more year."

Her mother stirred the pot as the maize meal thickened. "That is enough. I don't want to hear anything more about it. You will do what your father says."

With the fresh confidence of her new-found faith, Kasoni realized she had a higher allegiance. Swallowing hard, she stood and faced her mother. "I cannot agree to this. It will not help me in my life." Combined with her traumatic childhood memory of the circumcision ritual was the realization that it was something that could not be part of her Christian faith.

Her parents were aware that her routine church attendance had suddenly become something more meaningful to her. They knew the church's stand against many of the traditional rituals but were firm in their determination that their daughter would become a woman and undergo female circumcision as demanded by their tribe.

Somehow Kasoni was aware of God giving her courage to stand up for what she believed. As she shared her story with another Christian girl in her year at school, they encouraged each other to resist the pressure to undergo the ritual. Kasoni tried to explain her position to her siblings.

"In my culture, my younger siblings were not supposed to undergo the cut before me because I was older than them, but I told them my position and explained that I was not going to do it. I told my younger sister that she was welcome to join me in my stand against circumcision, but my brother would have to undergo it because he was a boy. Even though my brother did not understand everything about the culture at that time, he knew he had to undergo it."

Kasoni made her position clear to her brother. "OK, please do not wait for me to come home and say I am going to undergo the cut, because I am not going to do it."

Outraged and publicly embarrassed at a daughter's challenge to his authority, her father summoned Kasoni and made his feelings clear.

"This is the time when you have to undergo the cut in order to be a real woman in the community and to be accepted. If you continue to refuse, you will not be allowed to attend any community or family meetings; you will not even be informed about family matters; you will be an outcast because you have not followed your culture. You know very well that all Samburu women are undergoing the cut."

The family made all the initial preparations for her circumcision, insisting that she should undergo it. Kasoni, however, was determined to maintain her position, even if it meant losing her life, which was always a possibility. At that stage, she was oblivious to the physical consequences of female genital mutilation, normally referred to as FGM. Rather than concern about the physical effect on herself personally, her resistance was born of a deep-seated belief that this whole ritual was not of God. She could not shake off the sense of inhumanity that she had experienced watching it as a young girl.

As her father had said, she was aware that all Samburu girls were undergoing it, from Standard 5 onwards. She knew that some girls actually asked their parents for it because of their desire to be seen as grown-up and accepted as real women in the community. By the time Kasoni reached Standard 8, her final year in primary school, her peers began to make fun of her as they went home together after school.

"You are walking with big people and you are still a young girl because you have not had the cut." Kasoni tried to laugh them off and pretend she didn't take them seriously. It actually wasn't a big issue for her because she knew what she wanted in life. Her heart was set on a greater dream; her desire was to follow God and fulfil his plan wherever he led her. Aware of the cultural importance of the whole matter, however, and of the battle being waged against her, she prayed constantly, "God, you called me with a purpose in this Samburu land. Protect me now from those who would plot against me."

She believed firmly that God had put it in her heart to stand against FGM, not just on her own behalf but for the sake of other girls in her community. Her Christian faith and attendance at church made the battle more public; people were aware that FGM was not encouraged there and saw the church as being against their culture.

While Kasoni was still in Standard 6, an older Christian friend from the church, aware of the stress she was under, invited her to come and stay with her family. Delighted to have Christian support, Kasoni moved from her cousin's house. A Maasai married to a Samburu, this woman knew something of the struggle Kasoni was facing and was able to support her and pray with her in her stand against it. Throughout Standards 7 and 8 at school, Kasoni found refuge in the home of this friend.

The battle, however, continued. At the age of fifteen, she completed her primary education and moved on to Form 1 of secondary school. She was now well past the usual age for circumcision and her father continued to demand, via her mother, that she come home for the ceremony. Kasoni knew they were humiliated to have her refusal publicly known and to have to admit her uncircumcised status.

She was conscious of both sides of the issue. "When a girl is circumcised, they say, 'Our child now no longer has a stain.' They think of a circumcised girl as 'clean' and 'beautiful'. On the other hand, I looked on that ritual as a covenant because circumcision is a shedding of blood. It seemed to me as if they were making a covenant with their forefathers and, after doing that, those spirits would still be following me. As a Christian I could not do that because I did not know what kind of covenant they were making. Jesus has taken my sins away and I don't need any other blood to cleanse me. That is the only covenant I want."

She had to be careful how she talked about it. "The only way to escape was to keep on postponing. They could do anything if I didn't agree with what they had decided; if I refused outright, they could take me by force and circumcise me. It is normally done by women but if you don't undergo it voluntarily the young men will hold you and do it by force. Up to now I have been protected; I thank God for that."

Sometimes Kasoni, afraid to go home in the holidays, found herself with nowhere to stay. When she explained that she had refused FGM, her relatives refused to accept her into their homes. At one point, almost at the end of her tether, she thought she would have to try to survive in the bush. The pressure from those around her was relentless, even from some of the church leaders, who said, "The Bible says you should obey your parents." Yet Kasoni refused to give in.

"I was very serious about it. I told them, 'The Bible says, "Obey your parents *in the Lord* (Ephesians 6:1)."' That is a very different thing."

During the school holidays, she attended the youth camps held in Tuum and, when the week was over, normally stayed with friends from church instead of returning to her family in South Horr. Sometimes she went to stay with Stephen and Angelina, who had lived in Tuum for many years.

At the end of her final primary-school year, she planned to stay with them again, but discovered they were on leave. Two other missionaries, Paul and Elizabeth, who were looking after the place in their absence, took her in and befriended her. Delighted by their offer to cover her secondary-school fees, Kasoni started at Maralal Girls High School the following term. Her joy at reaching secondary school soon dissolved, however, when she was recognized by girls from her home place who knew she had not undergone FGM. Making her the focus of their jokes, they accused her of dishonouring her clan and shaming her family. Worn down by their attacks, she returned to Tuum in the holidays and shared her situation with Stephen and Angelina, now back from leave.

"It was a breakthrough. They listened to my story, they affirmed my stand against FGM, they welcomed me into their family, and I have been staying with them ever since. They are my adopted family."

The situation with her own family continued to deteriorate. In the face of her father's insistence that she go home for the ceremony, the only thing she could do was stay away from her village. There was no way she could go back into the situation without the risk of forcible FGM. For three years she did not see her parents, staying at boarding school in term time and spending the holidays with Stephen and Angelina or other friends.

One day, however, she decided that, despite the risk, she ought to go and see her mother. Stephen provided a vehicle and a driver and four young Christian men from the church who went with her for protection. Her family welcomed all these visitors to the village, realizing they could do nothing by force in the circumstances. The visit lasted about an hour, during which everyone was given a cup of tea and engaged in conversation, but beneath the surface was the constant awareness of danger; at the slightest sign of aggression, they were ready to take off. Kasoni's mother was glad she had come but her father refused to see her. His message to her was, "You will never call me father until you leave the church you are in and give up your refusal to be circumcised."

Kasoni is realistic about the threat. "My father was known in the village as being aggressive and fierce. People were saying, 'How brave you are to resist him.' I know my father can come with a knife but I usually don't fear that knife. I just wait for it. If he comes near me, I will be protected." Looking into the distance, she admits her father is not the only danger. "Other guys who want to circumcise women go around harassing you. They will tell you they can make sure you will not live. But now it's in God's hands."

During her second year in secondary school, she faced a new challenge. One day she was travelling in a large vehicle full of children, some of them from her Sunday-school class. When the steering failed without warning, the vehicle suddenly left the road and rolled over three times. People and objects were thrown around inside the vehicle before it came to a stop on its side, with Kasoni at the bottom of a heap of bodies. Some of the children panicked immediately, scrambling out of the vehicle and taking off into the bush; some were calling Kasoni's name, others were ominously still. The last to emerge from the wreckage, Kasoni did not know what to do first: try to help the injured or run after those who had fled. Two of the boys were already dead. Thirty minutes passed before a vehicle appeared and took the most seriously injured to hospital. Over the following year, needing treatment for her physical injuries and counselling after the trauma, Kasoni was in and out of hospital and missed much of the school year.

At the same time, pressure concerning the issue of FGM continued to mount, both from home and from the girls at school. Her father sent a message: "Go away from here. You are no longer my child. I will not count you as mine." Her mother had quietly begun to support her, although she had no power to do anything about it. She herself was being harassed, her husband blaming her for encouraging Kasoni in her rebellious stance.

Depressed and hopeless, Kasoni felt unwanted and rejected by her family; even her brothers did not want to see her, vowing never to speak to her again. She began to wonder if her determination to go against the tide of her culture was worth it.

"People said I was cursed by my father because of my attitude to FGM. The story of the accident grew until a message reached my parents that I was dead. My father was relieved that his problems were solved and rebuked my mother for being upset. 'You'd better cry for the other children but not for Kasoni,' was his comment."

Looking back, Kasoni sees God's hand in it all. "I did not die but lived to testify to how good God is. They were afraid when they eventually saw me again because they had thought I was dead. They began to realize that God was protecting me."

Battered by the physical and emotional storms she had been through, Kasoni found refuge in the home of Stephen and Angelina. "They took care of me and gradually I realized I was secure and loved and protected. They have been my nearest parents, taking care of me, paying my school fees and for my personal needs, praying with me, and showing me the love of Jesus. I thank God for them and for all they have done for me."

As part of her recovery process, Kasoni transferred to

a school in Murang'a, closer to Nairobi, away from the taunts and jeers of the Samburu girls who knew her. She grew as a Christian, becoming a Christian Union leader and prayer co-ordinator. In 2009 she completed her secondary education and returned to Tuum to help in the church and especially in the youth camps, which had been such an encouragement to her as a young Christian. Spending six months at the Discipleship Training School run by Youth With a Mission in Athi River, near Nairobi, helped her to mature further as a Christian and equipped her as she took part in outreach among her own people and among the Turkana.

At the beginning of 2011, she was accepted by a college in Nairobi to study for a Diploma in Community Health and Development. She is excited about the possibilities this will open up.

"I am enjoying my studies; this is my career. The main reason I want to do this course is to go back to Samburu land to share the word of God and offer help to my community. I have a vision to go into primary schools and deliver the message about FGM to young girls who have not already been pressurized into it. They have no idea of the implications. They need to know the extent of the operation that is done, the huge scar that is left, the ongoing suffering they will endure in the coming years as a result of it. They need to know that it can involve prolonged bleeding, infections, infertility, and even death, and that, whatever happens, the experience will haunt them for the rest of their lives."

On the other hand, Kasoni acknowledges that girls also

need to have a realistic knowledge of what is involved in refusing FGM. According to Samburu culture, men do not marry uncircumcised girls. In the unlikely event that such a thing should happen, the boy's parents would make sure the girl was circumcised later, even after she had had children. Kasoni tells me of an uncircumcised Turkana girl who was married by a Samburu. Last year in Tuum, while giving birth to her fourth child, she was circumcised by force.

At the age of twenty, Kasoni is already old when it comes to availability for marriage.

"Some Christian Samburu men congratulate me for what I have decided but, despite that, they will not marry someone who is uncircumcised. The clan's feelings are strong and they find it very hard to take themselves out of that situation. I would probably have to marry someone from another tribe."

As her father predicted, Kasoni's stance has distanced her from her family.

"I went home and found my younger sister married when she was fifteen, having had very little opportunity to go to school. It was a traditional marriage so I wouldn't normally attend, but they didn't even tell me about it till it was too late."

It is not just her family's attitude that saddens her, however. She grieves for all that her younger sister has missed in life.

"When she was fourteen, that sister had a child by someone else. Some girls have children from the age of twelve onwards. People say circumcision reduces the chance of having children young. But after FGM at twelve or thirteen, girls are told they are grown up. Both boys and girls start boasting and feel they can do anything they want now they are circumcised; they are big people who don't need to take heed of anybody. Can you imagine a girl of twelve or thirteen years when she is told she is a grown woman now in the community, just because of FGM? What are they doing actually? They are destroying their lives." Kasoni's eyes light up with passion as she dwells on the fate of the young girls in her tribe.

In recent years, a few other girls in the area have begun to take a stand against FGM and over the past year, attitudes in Kasoni's family have gradually softened towards her.

"Thank God, things have started changing now. My father still finds it difficult but he is not as aggressive as he was. Life has been hard for him. Over the years, some of his camels and cattle have been taken by Turkana raiders and some died in the drought, leaving him these days with a depleted herd of goats. My mother is showing me her love and has been supporting me. I thank God for her. I can go home now and my father will accept me even though he does not agree with what I say. He can see I am at college and am doing well. He is growing older and some of his children do not remember him, but I go and visit and give them what I can because they are not working. They realize I care for them."

Kasoni sees that if she is to have any hope of doing the work she dreams of among her people, she needs government backing, which in theory she already has. The Kenya Prohibition of Female Genital Mutilation Bill 2010 states that anyone convicted of practising FGM will be sent to jail for seven years or fined KES500,000. Anyone who causes death in the process of carrying out FGM will be liable to life imprisonment. Those convicted of aiding, abetting, or carrying out FGM will be liable to imprisonment for a term of between three and seven years or a fine of between KES100,000 and KES500,000.[2]

Yet the practice continues. Government laws are often treated with less respect than cultural values, so local leaders can take their daughters through the ritual and turn a blind eye to the law, reinforcing cultural values in the eyes of their people. Perhaps government legislation would be easier to implement if it were accompanied by education and awareness-raising exercises on the ground, such as envisaged by Kasoni. She longs to see women given the opportunity to examine conflicting attitudes to FGM and ultimately delivered from its damaging physical and psychological effects.

"I understand Samburu culture and as a Samburu I can explain the consequences, but I can also let young girls know they don't have to do it. I want to share my own experience and set an example as a Christian woman. I want them to see I am still alive and healthy and looking towards the bright future God has for me."

It is not only the Samburu who practise FGM. The World Health Organization estimates that between 100 and 140 million girls and women worldwide have been subjected to some form of the operation. Estimates based on the most recent data indicate that 91.5 million girls and women above nine years old in Africa are currently living with the consequences of FGM.[3]

Kasoni and I sit back and relax as Brian brings us coffee and *mandazi*. As the three of us talk and laugh together, we are aware of a bond that transcends our different backgrounds: the oneness in Christ that we have experienced so many times on our journey. I look across at Kasoni, glowing with her love for God and her concern for Samburu women, a thrilling example of the transforming power of the gospel in this land. Tomorrow I will hear a very different story.

9
Nabiki

The silver pieces and white shells on Nabiki's headdress tinkled softly as she shook with fear. In the quietness of the early morning she had been left alone briefly in her mud house. Very soon the women would come and remove her headdress to shave her head in preparation for her Maasai wedding later that day. Once the celebrations were over, she would be living in her husband's village, away from her home and family. It was as if it were happening to someone else; it was all beyond her control.

She did not really know the man she was to marry but she had seen him a few times and knew he was very old – her sister said he was about sixty. He already had five wives, and at twelve years old she knew she would not be popular with them as his newest and youngest wife. She had heard that, like many men, he beat his wives when he was drunk or angry. The thought of leaving the safety of her mother's house terrified her. What would happen to her baby brother Simel, whom she had cared for every day since he was born? He would not understand where she had gone. She gave an involuntary sob of fear.

How had it all happened so quickly? Just four weeks

ago, in the month of December, she had been playing happily with the other children in the *manyatta* when her mother came and told her it was time for her to undergo "the cut". She closed her eyes and tried to block out the events that followed but it was impossible; she still felt the searing pain of burning flesh as the hot knife, sterilized in the fire, cut into her. The physical pain of that day had not gone away. The wound was still large and raw, making walking difficult and going to the toilet extremely painful. As a young girl she had known that she would undergo circumcision and accepted it as a necessary part of growing up. But how could she become a wife so soon? Usually girls had about a year to heal before they got married. She knew her family were poor and short of food; they needed the gifts they had received for her dowry. She also knew her husband wanted her immediately. She would have to get married sometime, but she was not yet ready to be a wife and she was afraid of this man. If they would only wait for a while, maybe she could get married later.

Her thoughts turned again to the mission compound where her cousins had gone last year. Threatened with marriage, they had both run away at night and taken refuge in the mission, where an Irish couple called Gary and Mary looked after them and helped them get places in school. Having started a church nearby, Gary and Mary had been to Nabiki's home many times, visiting the family when they were in the area. When her uncle was sick, they took him to the dispensary, and during the drought they brought food for the family. Many people knew them because of their work with schools throughout the area; in the nursery schools they distributed clothes and blankets and those funny little furry objects they called "teddies" that people in their country made for the children.

If only she had the courage to do what her cousins had done. She knew that Gary and Mary had protected them. She remembered the story she had heard of the rescue of another young girl the year before. This girl had been taken to a man who had had many young brides who had run away when they were about sixteen because of the abuse they were suffering. Someone in the girl's family came and pleaded for help, so Gary and Patrick, a Kenyan work colleague, went and retrieved her before any ceremony took place. Weighing up all she knew about Gary and Mary, Nabiki thought that if she could get to them, they would be kind to her.

The opportunity to go to school instead of going with this man she was supposed to marry suddenly seemed a very attractive option. Would it be possible? Could she make it to the mission if she tried? It was about three kilometres away and this early in the day it would be difficult to remain unseen. There was a track that vehicles used but it was too obvious; she would have to go through thick bush to avoid capture, and risk meeting the elephants and buffalo that roamed the area. She had only a few moments to decide; they would all be back very soon to continue the wedding preparations.

Quickly she removed her headdress, the important status symbol showing she had been circumcised. As she dropped it on the ground she left with it her commitment to the ways of her tribe and ran from the *manyatta*.

"Are you going to the mission?"

Too late. Her sister had seen her and guessed where she was going.

"Yes. I don't want to be married. I want to go to school."

"You can't go, Nabiki. Your wedding is today. The dowry is paid and everything is prepared."

Not wanting to hear more, Nabiki turned and disappeared swiftly into the bush. She was now determined not to go through with the wedding. Ignoring the pain, she ran as quickly as she could in the direction of the mission. Thorns caught her clothes and cut her feet, but she was barely aware of them as she concentrated on following as straight a path as possible to what had suddenly become her refuge. She had heard the stories. She knew her family would follow, perhaps with knives and spears, to reclaim her.

As she staggered into the mission, breathless and sobbing, she saw the white woman called Mary coming towards her, arms outstretched to support her.

"I don't want to get married today. I'm still raw from circumcision." Nabiki could hardly get the words out.

Quickly grasping the situation, Mary called for the gates to be locked.

"Don't worry, you're safe now. No one can harm you." Gently she helped the trembling girl into the house. As they sat close together on the sofa in the schoolroom, an uproar began at the gate. Nabiki's mother had arrived, demanding to see her daughter.

In the quietness of the house, Mary looked directly into young eyes full of fear. "Do you want to see your mother?"

Reluctantly, Nabiki nodded. How could she refuse to see her own mother?

As her mother stormed into the house with baby Simel tied to her back, Nabiki shrank back into the sofa, afraid of what was coming.

"What are you thinking? Are you trying to shame your whole family? Everything is prepared for the wedding. We cannot afford to cancel it now. Your husband will be embarrassed. How can we face the rest of the clan? Have you no shame? You are a disobedient, ungrateful girl."

As her mother launched into a diatribe against her, Nabiki curled up and sobbed gently.

"Crying is not going to help you. If you insist on having your own way and refuse to come with me, I am going to leave here now and kill myself because I can't face the shame of what you are doing. How will you feel then? I will be dead and you will have to get married anyway."

Upset by all the shouting, little Simel began to cry. It was the final straw for Nabiki, who loved both her mother and her brother dearly. She did not want to leave them but if she went with them now, her husband would take her away from them later.

"Please get Mum to leave," she cried to Mary.

"Enough." Mary stood up to confront the angry woman. "You are abusing the child and it cannot be allowed. You will have to leave."

Shouting and threatening, Nabiki's mother was escorted out of the compound, leaving a weeping Nabiki behind.

"It's not true; she won't kill herself," Mary tried to comfort the distraught child. "She is just trying to manipulate you to go back home."

Even if she did not carry out her suicide threat, Nabiki knew her mother would be beaten by her father when she returned home without her. The mother is always to blame if a child misbehaves. Was she right in bringing all this trouble on everyone? She sat on the sofa and continued to cry as she thought about her family and the way they had treated her. She loved her mother so much and yet her mother was trying to force her into this situation. The pain she felt at being cut off from her family and her home was almost too much to bear.

As she grew calmer, she realized that Mary was still there, available to comfort her.

"What do you want to do?" Mary asked her.

"I want to go to school where my cousins are. When I get there, I'll be safe and I can try to forget about it. I know I'm safe in here but my family are just outside the gates."

As she had guessed, her father had also come to the compound by this stage. She knew the men from the village could become violent very quickly. Gary, however, having been through this many times before, seemed to have the situation under control. Mary explained that Gary had already contacted the District Children's Office, the local Child Protection Agency in the main town of Narok, to alert them to the incident. They were on her side and would sort out the situation with her family. All she had to do was look after herself while others dealt with the legal side.

Mary helped her out of the rags in which she had arrived, so that she could wash and get dressed in clothes from a supply kept for such occasions. As Nabiki sat down to lunch with Mary's family, admiring her new clothes, she felt peace settling like a soft blanket over her bruised spirit. She felt protected and cared for. So much had happened in one morning: it all felt unreal, but perhaps Gary would be able to sort things out; perhaps things would work out alright in the end.

In the afternoon she went with Gary and Mary to the local primary school, about eight kilometres from the mission. Run by the government, the school takes day pupils but also offers boarding for those who live at a distance. Nabiki knew that children coming from the mission usually boarded for their own safety, as families would not risk taking them out of school by force.

Nabiki had never been to school before. Standard 1 had very young children, so she would go into Standard 2, where many of the girls from the mission started. She knew that her cousins who had started school the previous year were now in Standard 3.

As she went into the school office, she noticed a blackboard on the wall showing the number of girls and boys in each class. In Standards 2 and 3 the girls outnumbered the boys, probably because so many girls came to school from the mission. However, the girls seemed to drop out of school very quickly and by Standard 8 there were only a few of them in the class. She knew that by that stage many of the girls were married or had children. Once they were circumcised, the girls were regarded as women, regardless of their age. Nabiki hoped she would be able to stay in school for a long time.

One month later, having left the situation to settle for a while, Gary, accompanied by the local chief, went to Nabiki's home for the first formal meeting with her father. As they talked together, her father gradually became aware of the fact that if he did not comply with legislation and if his treatment of his daughter was considered wilful abuse, the District Children's Office could, through a decision made by the court, sell his animals, his land – if necessary everything he owned – in order to put his children through school. He could also face a prison sentence.

As the first school holidays approached in April, rumours began to circulate in the community that Nabiki would be married when she went home for the Easter break. Gary and the local chief went again to her home. As they read her father the legal rights of the child and underlined the repercussions if he did not adhere to them, he agreed that she would not be married against her will. He signed the necessary forms to that effect and agreements were formalized between the family and the mission and between the family and the government. All these forms would be kept in the District Children's Office in Narok.

During the first week of each school holiday, three times a year, Gary and Mary ran a Bush Bible Club for the children, where they played games, listened to stories, and shared snacks together. Catching the excitement of a special time of fun, Nabiki looked forward to attending with the other girls from school. Many from the community, even those who did not like church, came to the Bush Bible Club to watch the children play games and listen to the children's talk. The tug of war was a particular success.

On the Fun Day, when parents were welcome to attend and participate, Nabiki was delighted when her mother turned up. Her joy turned to embarrassment, however, as her mother began to abuse her in front of everyone.

"You bring shame on our family. You need to leave here now and come home immediately."

Taken aback and afraid of what this demand might mean, Nabiki refused to go with her. "I am doing well in school and want to stay here. I like the Bible Club. I don't want to go home."

Nabiki's mother was infuriated by her refusal to co-operate. Nabiki, realizing the depth of her mother's anger towards her, was deeply troubled. She knew that some Maasai mothers were even more traditional than the fathers in their beliefs. What happened to them had to happen to their children. One girl she knew, whose father did not want her to undergo FGM, was taken secretly to another area to be circumcised because her mother was adamant she could not be a woman without a circumcision ceremony.

Nabiki talked to Gary about her fear of returning home for the remainder of the holidays.

"What happens if they arrange the wedding again? They might not let me come back to school."

Gary was reassuring. "Your father has signed a legal agreement that protects you. He will not risk contravening that. You can come back here to the mission at any time if you feel under threat."

Nabiki knew that some children, whose families were still hostile, spent their school holidays at the mission; it was a haven that they continued to use until the chief was able to establish their safety at home. Struggling to trust Gary's judgment, and still anxious about the outcome, she returned home after the Bible Club. To her relief she found that, despite her mother's animosity, her father was now reconciled to the legal implications, and the holidays passed without incident. Her mother asked permission for Nabiki to return to school a day late as she needed her help and, when that was allowed by the school, it helped to introduce an element of co-operation and improved the relationship.

As the school year progressed, Nabiki's father heard reports that she was doing well in her studies and had been presented with a prize at the mission. For perhaps the first time, he was proud of his daughter and had to acknowledge the totally foreign concept that a girl could do well in school. He struggled to come to terms with such a new idea. Up to that time he had thought of girls only as a commodity to be owned or traded for a dowry. They were for collecting firewood, getting water, getting married, preparing food for men, having babies, and keeping life moving. Why should a girl be educated? For what purpose?

Now, however, he was beginning to see that perhaps there was another way. Seeing Mary's activities in the community had been a revelation to him. When Mary advised a family about treatment for a sick child and the child recovered, he realized women could have knowledge and information. He knew that Mary cooked and taught the children and did what he considered a wife's job to be, but she was also educated and could read and write. Perhaps there was some value in this education of girls after all.

In the meantime Nabiki's faith began to grow. When

she first came to the mission, she said to Mary, "I prayed and asked Jesus to help me get here." Even though she had not known God in any real way before that point, she could see how he had helped her at the most critical moment of her life. As she attended the Bible Club she came to understand more about Jesus and continued to learn to trust him for her protection.

Nabiki is now allowed to go freely to school. Her father is not completely happy about the situation but he realizes that if he takes his daughter out of school the government will follow it up and he runs the risk of losing his property or going to prison. It has been a very difficult walk for Nabiki but she has finally come to the place of being reconciled with her family and allowed to continue her dream of going to school like other children.

This story is typical of the experiences of some young Maasai girls. The District Children's Office in Narok has listed Acacia Grove Mission as a safe house for children. Apart from places in larger townslike Narok, there is nowhere else in the huge Maasai Mara area for children to go for help. Recognizing that children are at risk and can even be killed because they have dishonoured the family, Gary and Mary make their home available until something more permanent can be sorted out for them. When there is more than one child, they stay in the guest house or hall at the mission, where Mary and a Maasai lady care for them.

Mary says, "Sometimes they just need a few nights until they can get into boarding school, or, in an extreme case, into a home. The mission is seen as an extension of the child protection work, helping the agency locate and protect children in the area. We sit on the Area Advisory Council and work with the agency in any way we can."

All children coming to the mission as a safe house are registered with the District Children's Office in Narok, and all the families involved have to make an agreement with the government that children will not be harmed in any way, that they will be kept in school, and that they will not be forced to undergo FGM or given as child brides. Almost 100 children are currently being supported at school and protected from threatened abuse.

It is more difficult if girls are already married and have run away from their husband because of abuse. When they are taken to school, even if only twelve or thirteen years of age, the response of some in the community will be, "She is married, she is a man's wife; she should be at home, not coming to school."

Not all cases end as happily as Nabiki's. One girl walked a long distance to the mission only to find that Gary and Mary were away; some of the helpers set out to take her to school, phoning Gary to ask him to contact the District Children's Office. About 360 metres from the school, the girl's family drew up in a car and jumped out. Threatening the mission personnel with spears, they chased after the girl, caught her, and beat her up there on the road. No one stopped to help – the cultural norm is not to interfere in a family matter. Having already been married once, as a child bride, this girl was being married off to someone else for a second time, still a child. Bundling her into the car, the family took her back home by force. The girl is still being followed up by the authorities and Gary and Mary, deeply moved by this case, are conscious that somewhere a child may be suffering untold abuse without any recourse to help.

Child marriage has been highlighted as a key development issue in many countries, an obvious breach of children's rights that raises serious health and education questions. Tracy McVeigh, social affairs editor of *The Guardian*, pointed out in June 2011: "Tackling child marriage successfully could affect everything from HIV prevalence to child mortality and gender inequality."[1] It is this knowledge, coupled with God's clear calling to the work, that spurs Gary and Mary on in their drive to protect the young girls in their area. They wholeheartedly believe that God has put them in this place to protect and defend the innocent and vulnerable in the face of oppression.

The power base among the Maasai lies with the *Laibons*, the prophets. Gary and Mary are aware that they are living in the midst of a spiritual battle, with people travelling great distances to their area of Olkinyiei in order to consult the true *Laibons* based there.

"People will go to local ones who dabble in magic for everyday concerns, but for major problems they will come a long distance to see the real ones, the *Laibons* who live beside us. They are the only ones who have had power handed down to them through their family. Even people from the tourist camps and lodges in Maasai Mara Game Park will come to collect our *Laibons* and take them to their tourist camps where they pay them to bless their business; they often stop with us to ask for fuel for their vehicles before they go back again."

Although not coming from a Christian viewpoint, the *Laibons* are interested in the spiritual world and some are keen to know about the Bible and its concept of God. Recently they held a large gathering, where Gary was given the opportunity to speak. In the course of his talk he outlined the Bible's picture of the God of Israel, highlighting the contrast with the god followed by the Maasai. At the end of the meeting some concluded, "We see that the God of Israel is powerful." One of the *Laibons* decided to follow Christ, giving up witchcraft and burning all his calabashes connected with it. He now helps out at the mission. Such encouragements shine like beacons in the midst of the surrounding darkness.

The next morning I drive with Naomi to Amani, a craft training and marketing project for marginalized women, based in the suburbs of Nairobi. The temperature is slightly higher today and, as we sit in the garden waiting for coffee, Naomi produces hand-sanitizing gel, which has just become available in the country. Having been very ill with typhoid last year, she is careful to take precautions. The traffic noise is reduced to a background hum behind the high hedge; the chirping of birds in the trees and the laughter of children on the climbing frame at the other end of the garden encourage us to relax in the sunshine. The arrival of warm muffins and coffee eases us into our conversation about Naomi's work and its impact on the lives of girls like Nabiki.

Naomi becomes animated as she talks about her passion for making the Bible relevant to children in their own culture. In conjunction with the local church, she has produced a Sunday-school curriculum for four- to six-year-olds across Kenya and is about to start on one for ten- to twelve-year-olds. When she heard about Gary and Mary's work with children in the remote Olkinyiei area, she was fired with enthusiasm to produce materials that would be suitable for that very particular situation.

Patrick was a trained primary-school teacher in Olkinyiei. A committed Christian, the only church was a long way from his home, so he was overjoyed when Gary and Mary set up Acacia Grove Mission. He worked with them from the outset and schools were the natural place for him to start.

With Naomi's expertise in education, she and Patrick got together to plan a series of lessons giving an overview of the whole Bible, aiming to give children a firm foundation in the gospel and an understanding of the Christian faith. The lessons related specifically to issues the children were facing, with each lesson thirty-five minutes long, planned to fit in with the school timetable.

Each Friday morning in schools across Kenya, the first lesson of the day is set aside for Programmes of Pastoral Instruction. Any teacher or recognized religious leader from the community can come into school to teach that lesson. For Patrick it was an opportunity to teach something outside the regular Christian religious education curriculum.

He started working with Standards 4 to 8, where the children were aged roughly eleven to fifteen. Through the lessons he and Naomi put together, he tackled issues such as female genital mutilation, child brides, children's rights, monogamy and polygamy, children outside marriage, HIV/

AIDS, and love and affection in marriage. The children were already being exposed to these things in their own culture and home life, so Patrick felt it was quite appropriate to discuss them in a school situation, from a biblical perspective.

Naomi reflects, "We particularly wanted to tackle children's rights in their culture. When children know their rights, they realize there is another option and they can run to the mission if they are under threat. If they don't know their rights and that the law in Kenya is supporting them, then they think they have to go along with what they are being told."

Patrick and Naomi produced the first series of ten lessons, starting from creation and moving through the stories in the book of Genesis, many of which had relevance to the Maasai culture. They concentrated on getting the children to discuss and act out the story to make it real. Each week Patrick encouraged the children to write down anonymous questions that could be discussed the following week, generating a number of queries they might not otherwise have had the courage to raise. Sometimes he separated boys and girls during the lessons but most of the classes were taken together. It was very important for boys as well as girls to be taught about issues such as FGM.

The first time that FGM was discussed, he asked the children at the end of the class, "What do you think about it?"

The whole class replied unanimously, "It's bad."

Patrick was encouraged. He recognized that it was only a start and that things look very different when children are under pressure from adults or peers at home, but at least they were thinking about the issues before the situation arose. The fact that the law was on their side now was key, but he recognized that it would be a long time before what was stated in law was accepted as the cultural norm.

Ideally, he wanted to teach Standards 1 to 4 as well, and so began alternating between the younger and older age groups. What he really needed was a team of volunteers willing to teach these lessons in all the schools in the area.

Patrick is now in the process of finding such a team; once they are available, Naomi will train them in presenting the material. The lessons are very different from the rest of the curriculum, interesting and interactive, with a variety of activities: colouring, writing, questions, and debate; discussion is encouraged to involve the young people actively in the issues. Patrick tries to bring in extra resource people so that the children can hear the message backed up by others they respect in the community.

Naomi realizes that, good as Patrick is, there is an urgent need for a female worker.

"Even seven- or eight-year-old girls can be circumcised, before they have any idea of the implications or realize that they have any choice in the matter. We are really crying out for role models for girls to emulate. Ideally it should be a girl who has resisted circumcision talking to them, rather than Patrick, but we don't have one yet. We continue to pray for someone to fill that role."

Most of the girls in school are not circumcised because when they have been circumcised they are taken out of school to be married. Once that happens, they have no hope of being educated any further. The family will already have planned the marriage and that is the end of their education. Male circumcision is seen in a totally different light, with the boys generally continuing at secondary school afterwards.

With Patrick's inside understanding of life as a Maasai, he and Naomi are able to write the lesson plans together, reflecting local culture and thought processes. It has been a growing process for each of them. The approach is always practical – how can we best get this concept across to the children? They use as much visual material as possible: as the children do not have the opportunity to see many pictures, a good deal of time is spent preparing appropriate visual aids.

Naomi recognizes the challenge that faces them.

"This work in education and awareness-raising gives hope for the next generation. We are in it for the long haul. We may not see a great deal of change immediately but eventually, over time, people will come to acknowledge the wrongs that are being done to women and the culture will change."

As we finish our coffee, I watch the little girls playing happily on the climbing frame. I think of their future and my heart lifts in prayer for the women of Africa.

10

Guyo

There are suspiciously few people around as we approach the check-in desk at Nairobi Airport and present the tickets for the next leg of our journey.

"I'm sorry, there is no flight to Malindi today," the lady behind the desk announces.

"But we have tickets." We wave them hopefully. "We're booked on a flight at 6.00 p.m. and it's on the departure screen as leaving on time."

"No, it's been cancelled. There's no flight until Thursday."

Thursday is two days before our return flight to Belfast.

"We can't wait till Thursday. Is there a flight to Mombasa?"

"Yes, there's a flight to Mombasa tonight. If you want to take that, we can put you up overnight in Mombasa and take you to Malindi tomorrow by minibus."

"Fine. We'll take it." Relieved to be heading in the right direction, we settle down with our books in the departure lounge and hope the rest of the journey works out as promised.

In the event, we have a smooth transition from Mombasa Airport to the beachfront hotel, where we manage to get something to eat before the restaurant closes for the night. Our room has all the comforts of a good hotel and next morning we join tourists from around the world to enjoy an early breakfast overlooking the palm-lined white beach and blue waters of the Indian Ocean. Pleasant though it would be to stay, we board our minibus with a small group of travellers, European and African, who have likewise been diverted via Mombasa, and head north along the coast towards Malindi.

The temperature is distinctly higher than it was in Nairobi, or indeed anywhere else on our trip so far. The road runs through coconut palms, permitting an occasional glimpse of landscaped hotel gardens and turquoise swimming pools; at roadside stalls, women in brightly coloured *kangas*[1] sell their tomatoes and mangoes for a few shillings. The roofs of small mud houses provide a template for the soaring thatched hotel roofs appearing from time to time above the trees. Barefoot children wander around crumbling buildings bearing euphemistic "School" or "Supermarket" signs. Along the sides of the road the ubiquitous goats and chickens pick their way, somehow avoiding the *matatus*[2] and hotel minibuses constantly flying along the coast.

In Malindi we stroll along the busy street. Elegant Italian women in sunglasses and high heels mingle with their Muslim counterparts, heads covered by the hijab or completely enveloped in the burqa. Cheery drivers call out invitations to make use of their *tuk tuks*, the three-wheeled motorized rickshaws that transport people around town. Outside a number of shops we see signs for M-PESA, a mobile-phone money system set up by Safaricom, an affiliate of Vodafone. Less than three years old, it now has 7 million customers, making a huge impact on the economy as people transfer money with ease from one end of the country to the other.

In the Karen Blixen coffee shop, central meeting place of the town, we meet our friends Eddie and Mary, recently arrived from Ireland to work on the Galana project, three hours' drive away. Their situation, in the throes of setting up home in Malindi, brings back memories of our own arrival in Kenya many years ago and the struggles of adjustment to life in a culture so exciting yet so different from our own.

Later, on the shady veranda of our apartment, we keep hydrated with cold drinks as Derek, a farmer from Donegal, tells us how his work in this part of Kenya began.

"In 1998, Linda and I arrived with our two girls in Nyeri, about 160 kilometres north of Nairobi, to establish Honi Training Farm – an initiative aimed at improving the practical skills of local farm workers." Derek refills his glass and relaxes back in his chair as he reflects on their early days in Kenya.

"Our nearest European neighbours lived about twenty minutes' drive away. They had lived for a number of years with their young son and daughter in Galana, an area near Malindi, and had a real burden for the community there. As I shared my vision for agriculture in Kenya, dreaming of what could be achieved through working with local farmers, Tony and I discovered a mutual interest in exploring how we might help the Galana community."

On 3 January 2001 Derek and Tony drove into Galana for their first community meeting with the local people. It was a depressing experience.

People gathered slowly, reluctant to look these visitors in the eye. With the setting up of Tsavo National Park in 1948, they had been expelled from their homes and had settled on the Galana side of the park boundary. As the meeting proceeded they explained that the nearest school was twenty-five kilometres away and the nearest clinic was thirty kilometres in the other direction, on the other side of the Galana River. They felt like a forgotten people, had no idea who their Member of Parliament was, had never seen a councillor.

"We are hunters, but if we get caught hunting we are imprisoned. We are not farmers; we don't know how to farm and there is no one to show us. Most years we depend on famine relief food for seven months of the year. We can't see any way out of the situation – we're trapped here."

As Derek wrote up his report for the church, his heart was moved by the unbelievable poverty he had witnessed, the poor housing, the dearth of facilities, the lack of hope. When the church asked him if he would consider going to Galana, to set up a project there, he and Linda thought and prayed about it, recognizing the remoteness of the area and the difficulties it entailed. As they prayed, they felt a strong sense of call to the community in that region and agreed to go.

At this point, they discovered that Linda was pregnant again and decided to return to Ireland for the birth of their third child, after which they would come back to start the work in Galana. Michael, Tony's eighteen-year-old son, planned to spend some time with them there, finding out more about the people of Galana, their culture, and the challenges they were facing.

Their friends issued an invitation. "You folks have been so busy. Why don't you come and stay with us for a few days before you go back to Ireland? If you come for the weekend you can go to Nairobi on the Monday."

This sounded like a good plan, which Derek and Linda gratefully accepted, little knowing what lay ahead. To their utter shock and disbelief they arrived at the house to be greeted by the news that young Michael had been killed by a hippo.

Derek and Linda were stunned, unable to take it in. They were still speechless when Tony made a request to Derek.

"You knew Michael well and we've known you for a long time. Would you conduct the burial service for us?"

Derek was taken aback. He said, "Tony, I want you to know I have never done anything like this before. However, I said I would do anything I could to help and if you feel strongly that you want me to do it, then I'll try."

As the family gathered, Derek started to prepare the talk for the funeral service.

"Every time I sat down to think about it I broke down and cried. Linda and I wept our way through the preparation. We really struggled to get our heads round it but eventually I took the verse from John 3:16: 'God so loved the world that he gave his only Son.' Leading that service was one of the most difficult things I have ever had to do, and yet it was an honour to be asked to perform such a role for this lovely family."

The following day, as Derek and Linda left to go to Nairobi, Tony held Derek's hand tightly. "You're leaving us just when we need you most."

Derek said, "Tony, we're coming back. We've got this project to do that Michael was so interested in. Because he had such a passion for the Galana community and his life has now been cut short, it has made the call for us to go and help these people even more urgent."

A trust fund was set up in honour of Michael, with proceeds going to help the Galana community development. It remains as an ongoing witness to Michael's memory and the beginning of the Galana story.

In conjunction with people from the local church, Galana Community Development Committee was set up, working with fourteen villages, seven on each side of the river. Within weeks of Derek's arrival in Galana, an elderly man went missing after going to wash himself in the river. Local people suspected that he had been taken by a crocodile. A few days later, they discovered his head about a kilometre downstream on the other side of the river. As Derek talked to people about the incident, they shared stories of those they knew who had been taken by crocodiles, about children who had disappeared, about women with deformed arms who had been grabbed by a crocodile while drawing water from the river.

One day, not long after this incident, as they walked to a village, Derek heard two young children shouting on the far riverbank. A young boy on Derek's side of the river waded over to meet them and help them back across the river. In a practised routine, they took off their trousers, put them in a plastic bag, and held them on top of their head while they stepped into the water. As they crossed, the smaller children were up to their necks in the river, just managing to keep their heads above water. Derek was appalled at the danger they were in and realized they needed a bridge over the river. He turned to the people with him.

"Why are these children crossing the river?"

"They are going to school."

"Is there no school nearby on their side of the river?"

"No, the nearest school is about twenty-five kilometres away."

Derek had known they needed a school but he hadn't realized it was that kind of need – that they were willing to put their life at risk to get an education. He felt totally powerless as he watched them crossing the river and imagined one of these children being grabbed by a crocodile at any moment.

Exploring the best way of tackling the problem, Derek went to talk to the Kenya Wildlife Service (KWS) warden in Malindi. The assistant warden, Tuda, and a couple of rangers went with Derek to meet the community in Galana and talk about all the different wildlife problems they were experiencing.

Hearing the situation, Tuda shook his head. "We were

just not aware of this. We had no idea of the amount of hardship suffered by this community. Where human life is in danger, we have to take the initiative and dispatch these animals. That is always the case; we respect the sanctity of human life and if there is that amount of danger then we have to take action."

Derek was keen to get involved. "As a young lad I shot rabbits at home and am conversant with large-bore rifles. I have experience in animal control in Wildlife and Parks at home in Ireland. Is there any way I could assist you in shooting these crocodiles?"

The warden was amused. "You want to shoot a crocodile?"

"I don't *want* to shoot a crocodile, but I *do* want to help the community."

On the firing range, the warden was impressed by how Derek acquitted himself.

"Have you been militarily trained?" he asked.

"No," Derek smiled.

"IRA?"

"Definitely not."

"Will you accept the responsibility of being an honorary warden?"

Derek's name was put forward for selection and he was duly appointed, with the duties and powers of any KWS warden: powers of arrest, power to set up road blocks, power to direct the local rangers. During his years as warden in Galana, Derek carried out a Problem Animal Control exercise every few months, usually at the request of the local community. Accompanied by local rangers, always aware of the risk from Somali poachers who were heavily armed with automatic weapons, he would seek out the problem animals, ideally as they emerged from the water at dusk. It was not what he had envisaged when he signed up as a mission partner, but he was happy to do anything he could to protect this community that was fighting for survival.

In a meeting with the Tsavo KWS, Derek explained his desire to look at various aspects of the Galana community: education, agriculture, medicine, primary health care, and spiritual life. The community warden in Tsavo agreed to come and meet the people, so that together they could discuss what they wanted to do. Taking out a notebook, he drew an outer circle and an inner circle, with spokes going out from the centre.

Turning to Derek he said, "These spokes represent the various aspects of your work – education, agriculture, medicine, the building of the church – but it all comes from God. Never forget to keep God in the centre. Go ahead and follow whatever way you feel God is leading. I will assist you in any way I can."

Derek couldn't believe it. He'd had no idea the warden was a Christian.

He comments, "When you move into a new area, you get these confirmations at times that you are really in the right place."

Derek began to write down what he was seeing and send emails to a few folk he knew. One farmer from his home area in Donegal wrote back, "This is a horrendous situation. How much would it take to build a school?" At a rough estimate, Derek reckoned it would take around £20,000. "Give me the bank details," was the email reply immediately. "The money is yours."

The initial plan was to build four classrooms in one year, another block of four classrooms in the second year, and then hopefully a clinic in the third year. Before they knew it, they had raised £40,000 and were able to build everything in one year. As they started building they also wrote a proposal to the Irish overseas development charity GORTA, and received a quarter of a million euros to set up a four-year agricultural programme, training people in livestock-rearing, bee-keeping, crop-growing, and irrigation. Funds seemed to be pouring in.

Although the school was church-sponsored, it was a public facility. Derek went to the District Education Officer and asked if he could supply them with teachers. When they advertised, they managed to find a few teachers prepared to come to Galana.

Derek says, "Naomi was one of those who came at that time. She felt a strong sense of calling as a Christian teacher. She had lost her husband and was being harassed by his parents, who saw her son as their child. There was no regard for her as a woman. Coming to Galana meant she was out of their influence, and she found peace here." Having met Naomi in Ireland earlier in the year, I am interested to hear how she fits into the story. I am planning to meet her in a couple of days' time in Galana.

Once the school was built, on the north side of the river, Derek discovered they had created a reverse problem because children from the south side wanted to come to the new school, so they were still crossing the river every day. Derek was constantly aware of the need for a bridge.

The first step was to get a design that would work in Galana. The only possibility was a suspension bridge. They would have to build up towers from which to hang the bridge, as the banks were not high enough to hang it from one side to the other.

A contractor took measurements and obtained calculations. He came up with an initial figure of £25,000, which one church in Ireland raised almost immediately. As the project developed, however, the figures kept climbing until the final cost was closer to £150,000. Through an organization called Bridges to Prosperity, they found a design for a footbridge from a Swiss organization that had developed trail bridges in Nepal.

Although the initial research to find the right design and someone with the experience to build it took around six years, when work finally got under way it was completed in a year and was the longest suspension footbridge in Africa. One hundred and twelve metres in length, it contains over twenty-five tonnes of steel, five tonnes of steel rope, and 250 to 300 tonnes of concrete. Over 150 children now cross the bridge every day to go to school and when the river is in flood it is the only way for the community to obtain supplies, including post and medication.

Because of the generosity of so many donors there were funds remaining at the end of the project, so Derek went back to the community.

"What would you like to do with the rest of the

money?" he asked. "Should we extend the school, or start a different project?"

The response was unanimous. "We would like another bridge. This one has transformed our life here. We need another one further up the river."

Derek comments, "Nearly half the money was raised for the second footbridge before the first one was finished. God doesn't do things by halves. Not one footbridge, but two."

Because of the remoteness of the location, Derek had set up a camp in Galana where he and other workers could stay. Sitting round the fire at night, he would talk with some of the young people who came to help, encouraging them to think about what they would like to do in life. It was difficult to find young people who had had a full education because of the lack of schools in the area. Some had completed primary school, but had no secondary-school education. One keen young Christian, Robert, decided to go to Rubati Teacher Training College. Another young lad then decided to do the same, and gradually a few trained teachers trickled back into Galana.

Derek was always networking to try to get more education and training for young people.

"When these young people go out of the area to study we are concerned about whether they will come back again. We always ask them, 'Do you really want to help your community? Will you commit yourself to coming back here for four or five years after you have completed your studies?' So far, they have all been committed to coming back."

Alongside the development work, the spiritual was

always a priority for the development committee. Three churches have been set up since work began in the area, one at Bombi, beside the school, and one on either side of the bridge, with the community in each instance keen to provide the land. An evangelist was sent for training to Muguga Lay Training Institute, near Nairobi, and a number of others attended Discipleship Training School. All the personnel in the project did Theological Education by Extension, coming at 6.30 in the morning to study together. Their desire was to keep God central.

Derek reflects, "People are determined to lift their community out of poverty. It is not all plain sailing but they still go on. When I am invited to the prize-giving day at the school, I am thrilled that we have come this far. I think back to that first meeting where not a member of the community could look me in the eye because they were so dejected and depressed. They are so different now – they have a pride in their community and in all they have achieved. With God's help they are looking forward to all he still has in store for them."

We leave Malindi at 8.30 next morning, five of us packed into Eddie's twin-cab pick-up. As we negotiate our way through the morning traffic – animal, pedestrian, and vehicular – initial comfort gives way to a jolting forecast of the road to come as we leave the tarmac for the dirt road leading to Galana Ranch. Deep unexpected potholes appear at random intervals, skilfully avoided by Derek, who swings the steering wheel, throwing us together in the back seat with a certain amount of hilarity. As the vehicle rocks from side to side, he casually identifies some of the birds that provide a backdrop to our journey: hornbills perched in trees, yellow bustard swooping overhead. The smallest of the antelope family, tiny dik-dik with their large dark eyes, dance like dainty ballerinas through the undergrowth, and further down the road taller elegant impala with their distinguishing markings lift their heads at our noisy intrusion of their space.

We leave the road, such as it is, and drive a short distance through the bush until the Galana River comes into view. We draw to a halt; having heard the stories, we regard the deceptive quietness of the murky water with respect. Derek dismounts first and approaches the riverbank with care, clapping his hands and making sufficient noise to ensure we have no unwanted animal company. As we stretch our legs along the water's edge, we watch a pod of hippos, large and small, splashing happily together near the far bank. It is difficult to imagine that they are one of the most aggressive creatures in the world and the most dangerous animal in Africa. We perch on the riverbank and enjoy our picnic, revelling in the beauty of our surroundings and thanking God for the unique privilege of being in such a place.

Back in the vehicle, we head once more for Bombi, centre of the Galana project. The road becomes progressively less distinguishable and I wonder how anyone knows how to find this place. Suddenly a gateway appears, opening onto prefabricated concrete buildings – a small church straight ahead and over to the left a long, low building that must be the school.

Welcomed with much enthusiastic handshaking, we are

given a tour of the complex and an introductory talk by the deputy headmaster in the school. People are excited to see Eddie and Mary, who have come to head up the work on the second bridge over the river. I am introduced to Guyo Jefferson, the young project manager who oversees the irrigation scheme, and, as the others continue to explore, we sit at a table in his office with a cup of tea.

"I am a member of the Watta people," he tells me with a smile. "We are a marginalized community who settled in Galana when we were forced out of our home place in Tsavo National Park. Two main groups of people, the Waliangulu and the Watta, have always been known as great elephant hunters in the whole Tsavo area."

Guyo and his twin brother grew up with their brother and four sisters in a small traditional village called Garisemke, in a remote area of Galana. His mother was the first of his father's three wives; the second wife also lived in the village with her four children, the third wife having left after a short marriage. Their father worked as a guide in a tourist lodge, a world away from the family home.

At the age of thirteen, the twins began their education at the closest primary school, which was around thirty-five kilometres away at Galana Agricultural Development Corporation (ADC). They boarded at school from Monday to Friday, returning home for the weekend.

One day while Guyo's mother was drawing water at the river, she was attacked by a crocodile and almost lost her right hand. Although the wounds eventually healed, she was left disabled, without the use of her arm and unable to carry out her usual domestic duties. With their sisters all married and away from home, Guyo's brother decided to leave school and stay at home to help his mother. He did what he thought was the best thing in the circumstances and got married while still young so that his wife could help his mother in the home.

Every Friday evening Guyo would walk from school to his home in Galana, making the return journey to school on Sunday afternoon. Sometimes he was fortunate enough to get a lift in a vehicle for part of the distance. After some time his brother managed to buy a bicycle on which he sometimes gave Guyo a lift back to school on Sunday. Because the land bordered the national park, there was always the possibility of meeting elephants, buffalo, or even lions on the way.

Guyo is philosophical about the risks with which they lived. "Our tribe knows how to behave with animals and how to avoid them or escape. One day we came across an elephant with calves, which can be very dangerous as she is protective of her young. She waved her ears to show she was angry, but we just kept cool and dashed from that place into the bush. We thanked God that he delivered us that day."

A local church leader saw the potential in this young man from the village and spent time with Guyo, reading the Bible to him and explaining God's love for him and God's plan for his life. Very soon, fifteen-year-old Guyo realized he needed to make a specific commitment to follow Christ for himself. While growing up, he had been conscious of an awareness of God within his family and a sense of awe towards him, but now he began to see God actually working in his own life. Trusting in this God who had reached out to him, Guyo persevered through his primary education despite his late start, and felt a great sense of accomplishment on finishing Standard 8.

During his late teens, Guyo began to pray that God would show him what he wanted him to do with his life. In his mind he had a secret dream of becoming a resource for his community, able to help people develop and move forward. He didn't know how that would happen but he kept praying that God would work through him and somehow bring it to pass.

Guyo finished primary school just as Derek came to Galana to set up the project. He did sufficiently well to get an offer from three secondary schools, but secondary education with its fees, uniform, and other costs, was beyond the family's means. With his mother, he travelled to Derek's camp at Galana to talk through the possibilities, wondering if this newcomer would have any ideas about the way forward. Derek was hopeful that someone would be able to help Guyo.

Guyo could not quite believe it. "It sounded like something extraordinary, that I should get help in this way, to be able to go to secondary school. I prayed so hard, 'God, please see me through. Let this happen.' At the same time I thought this must be God working through these people."

The following morning Guyo and his mother travelled with Derek to the tourist lodge along the river where his father was working. The English lady who owned the lodge took an interest in Guyo and agreed to pay for his secondary education. Not long afterwards he started Voi

High School, to the delight of Derek and the whole Galana community. Very few from the area managed to get to secondary school.

Guyo did well in Form 1, thrilled to have this amazing opportunity. One day when he was in Form 2, however, he was suddenly summoned to the school office and informed that he would have to leave, owing to unpaid fees. It was a huge shock because his sponsor had undertaken to pay the fees needed for all four years of secondary school. He didn't know where to turn.

"Because I always depended on God for everything, I immediately prayed, 'God, I don't understand what is happening. I believe you have a plan for my life. Please see me through this situation.'" His family and friends were likewise upset.

"Does this mean you are now out of the school for ever?"

"I don't know, but I know God is there. He must have an answer."

Guyo struggled to hold on to his faith in the God who had brought him this far.

Distraught, he telephoned Derek. "I have been sent home because my school fees didn't come."

Derek said, "It's not a big issue, Guyo. Don't worry; give me the details of the school and the headmaster, and I will call him. I will find the money one way or another to get you back into school. Meet me in Malindi and I will get you a cheque. God is with you and will help you through this. Don't worry about the money."

On telephoning the headmaster, Derek learned that

owing to difficulties between Guyo's father and the owner of the lodge, she had withdrawn her offer of help. Derek assured the headmaster that the fees would be paid and that Guyo did not want any disruption to his education.

That Sunday Guyo went to church in Malindi with Derek, who was speaking at the service. Suddenly Derek announced, "I have someone from Galana with me today. Come and tell us about your life, Guyo."

Guyo laughs now as he describes his shock at the invitation. "I was not good at speaking in front of an audience but I had to stand and greet the congregation. I talked about the challenges I was facing and why I was in Malindi. I shared my faith that God would provide what I needed. After the service people came and pledged their support. The following day I received a cheque to cover the whole year's fees. I prayed, 'O God, thank you. I was not expecting anything like this.' This was God. I kept praying and praising him for all he had done."

Guyo went back to school. Through the Galana project, his fees were paid and he persevered in his studies up to Form 4, doing well in his exams and working as a volunteer with the project during the holidays. When he returned home at the end of high school, Derek sat down to talk to him.

"Guyo, we have had a meeting of the community and they have chosen you to be assistant project manager. Would you be willing to take on that responsibility?"

Guyo did not have to think for long. "Yes, I believe God has given me this responsibility even though I am so young. He has had this in his plan, so I have to go ahead and do it and see the outcome. I will make it because God is with me."

Guyo could see the impact the project was already having on the health, education, and lifestyle of his people. He recalls some of the stories of those who had suffered because of the river in recent years. In an ironic juxtaposition of cultures, one man was killed crossing the river to get his mobile phone charged in the ADC centre on the other side. Few families were untouched by the threat of the river. One of Guyo's own sisters, a twenty-six-year-old mother with two children, was taken by a crocodile in 2002 while fetching water from the river. In the same year he lost another sister, who had three children, when she was killed by robbers breaking into her house. Two bereavements in one year was a heavy load for the seventeen-year-old to bear.

Guyo was concerned for the spiritual well-being of his family. He usually took his siblings with him to church, but his mother refused to accompany them.

"I can pray at home; why should I go to church?" she would reply when Guyo asked her to come with them.

"There is more to it than just praying at home," Guyo responded. "We need to involve God in every part of our lives. He has a perfect plan for us."

One Christmas Day she finally relented. "Today I have to go to church," she told Guyo.

"That day she got saved," he tells me with a wide smile, shaking his head in amazement. "She is now firm in her faith. That was five years ago."

At first, coming into such a big project straight from high school was daunting, but Guyo knew from personal experience how significant the project was going to be for the community. He kept trusting that the God who had led him into this work would be with him and equip him for the task. He knew that Derek and the local church were always on hand to encourage and advise when needed. They developed a strong sense of team spirit as they worked together.

An opportunity opened up for him to do a short course in project planning and management at the Training Centre of Management in Arusha, Tanzania. Coming straight from high school, conscious that he was the youngest in the class, Guyo was somewhat overwhelmed to find himself among older, more knowledgeable project managers, some of whom even had their own vehicles. However, he was welcomed warmly into the group.

"They were so kind to me, saying, 'Oh, young man, where are you coming from? Which project are you involved in?' I built up a very good relationship with them. I managed to learn much from those guys and have kept up a friendship with some of them to this day, visiting them in their home areas. I enjoyed learning so many things and the course really broadened my knowledge and understanding of development work."

Derek welcomed him back to the Galana development project at the end of the course.

"You can make it," he encouraged Guyo. "You have a heart to work with the community and you are developing all the time. Up to this time, you have been working as a volunteer, but now we want to employ you."

Guyo accepted this responsibility. "My life is to help the whole community. I want to do that in every way possible. I want to change things, physically, politically, spiritually." He was committed to the strengthening sense of call on his life.

One day Derek approached him again. "We want to send you to driving school. Are you ready for that?"

Guyo was excited. "Of course. Yes. That is the next stage."

When he completed his driving course in Malindi, he was the first person from Galana to be given a driving licence. He was now able to help drive the vehicles backwards and forwards to Malindi or around the site as needed.

A short time later, he was given the option of doing further studies.

He did not take long to consider it. "Since that dream of helping the community is still there, I will have to continue my studies, so that I can fulfil it more effectively."

"Which course do you think you can do?" asked Derek, keen for him to choose his own path.

"I will have to do something on community development and social work."

Together they discovered the Kenya Institute of Community Development and Social Work in Nairobi, where he could do a Diploma in Community Development. Since the project was paying his fees, he had to sacrifice his salary, but he understood that eventually both he and the project would benefit. Moving to Nairobi, he concentrated on his studies during term time, returning to pick up his work in Galana in the holidays.

Through all the ups and downs of the project and his studies, Guyo's prayer was always consistent: "God, I am trusting that if you have chosen me to change this community then you will help me to accomplish that."

One of the problems he had to deal with concerned students from Galana who found themselves in trouble when their fees were no longer covered. They started telephoning Guyo, at college in Nairobi, asking if he could help. Putting himself in their shoes, remembering his own struggles over fees in high school, Guyo made every effort to assist them. Researching to find a possible donor, he wrote a proposal for fees for six students and sent it off to the UK. He was delighted when he was informed that they had received the funding. He was gradually learning his way round the challenges of development projects.

In October 2010, Guyo's studies were coming to an end. Having completed his exams, his final task was to write up a project proposal. From his practical experience in Galana, he knew that the theory often did not match what worked out on the ground, but he had the advantage of working alongside the community while drawing up his proposal. He visited various government offices to do his research and ended up submitting one proposal to KWS for KES750,000 and another to GORTA for around 1 million.

Calling a team together, Guyo shared his vision for the way forward. "Donors like to test our capacity. They want to know how we will manage the project, how we plan to meet the goals stated in the proposal. How is the community going to work together if we get this sponsorship? We need to set up an office; we need a facility to carry it all forward."

Motivated by his enthusiasm, the team started working out their ideas without delay. A short time later they were delighted to hear that they had received half of the amount requested, on the understanding that the community would supplement what they received with their own contribution.

Guyo is conscious of the responsibility he shoulders in the project.

"Any issue that arises about education or any other matter in the community is referred to me. People here have known me since I was a child, so they trust me. Sometimes I feel overwhelmed and wonder how I can possibly deal with so many matters at once. But most of the time I understand that this is the realization of my dream all those years ago to become a support and resource to the community. What matters is that we are involved together in community development as change agents. We have to be flexible and adapt to the situation as we go along. Many may not understand the need to adjust their ideas and it is a challenge to talk to them and persuade them, but challenge is a part of life."

Last year, Guyo became very ill with suspected brucellosis, which was treated with a long course of injections. Further investigations, however, revealed stomach ulcers as the problem. Alongside medical treatment, the doctor advised a balance in his lifestyle. The combination of study and project responsibilities was affecting his health. The church leaders were supportive and encouraging, understanding his position but advising him to have wisdom in his work/life balance.

Guyo appreciates their partnership with him, recognizing his need of older, wiser heads.

"I am grateful for my mentors in so many areas. I have overcome those challenges through prayer. I eventually got the correct medicine and am feeling so much better. We have now started a second phase of the irrigation programme. I still keep my dream in mind. It will be realized through prayer and keeping close to God and to the community. With God, everything is possible."

Not long ago, Derek came to him and said, "The community have asked for a second bridge. Can you get the community together so we can meet them?" Guyo brought together the local chiefs, administration officials, councillors, anyone of influence, to discuss the construction of a second bridge. As they met with Derek and Eddie, people were positive and excited, enthusiastic about doing all they could to help.

Guyo is pleased that they are keen to take the project forward. "I will work with them. To mobilize the community, this is part of my dream. I want to encourage the community to pull together as much as possible. I do pray for that. Success depends on our ability, not on size, and I know that we will succeed because God is with us.

"Since that day long ago when I prayed that God would help me with my education, I have seen him helping me over the years to accomplish my goal – I first trusted him when I was fifteen and I am twenty-six years old now. Even though life has its challenges, we must put ourselves in God's hands. We can make it. I base my faith on the verse, 'Do not fear, for I am with you; I will uphold you with my righteous right hand' (Isaiah 41:10). When I read such a verse I know that God is always with me and I face the future with him."

Guyo's face glows with enthusiasm as he contemplates all that is possible in a future blessed and led by God. Committed to being part of that future, he is determined to realize his dream of improving life for his people. As I look out over the hot, barren landscape towards the green of the irrigation project, and reflect on the multitude of lives now touched by school, clinic, church, and bridge, it is thrilling to see the transformation taking place. No one knows all that God will accomplish through young men like Guyo, starting life with many challenges but totally committed to trusting him as they serve their community.

11

Naomi

"Naomi, are you sure you will be at home on Saturday? I am coming to do the introductions." Stanley hoped nothing would go wrong this time.

Naomi was too excited to entertain such negative thoughts. "Yes, don't worry. I'll be there; everything will be ready."

Eleven years earlier, finishing his final year of secondary school as a twenty-year-old, Stanley Kivulu had first declared his intentions to the parents of Naomi Mutinda Wambua. In an interview that demanded some courage, he had announced, "I love this girl and I pray that one day we will get married."

Her parents took a dim view of this bold young man who had suddenly appeared as suitor to their daughter. It was much too soon for him to be thinking of marriage to a fourteen-year-old first-former. As Christian parents, they wanted their daughter to complete her secondary education while she had the chance. It was good that the young folk were both from the Kamba tribe and had met through Christian Union activities at their respective schools, but let them wait a while before talking about such a serious commitment.

Naomi and Stanley had dutifully obeyed their elders. Gaining high marks in her Form 4 school examinations, Naomi had completed secretarial and computer courses and then found secretarial work in Nairobi. There was no way her parents could afford to send her to university. Meanwhile, Stanley had done further studies and found an engineering job with an Israeli firm in Nairobi, where he had worked for five years.

Having met up again in Nairobi, they were now ready to readdress the question of marriage with the family. On the pre-arranged day, Stanley brought his parents and the elders from his home place to meet Naomi's family. Surrounded by family members, he declared his desire to marry Naomi.

"These people have not just met in Nairobi. It's eleven years since I first heard my boy here talk of Naomi. They have been keeping quiet about it all this time." His mother surprised the elders by filling them in on the history of the young couple.

Having established that Stanley had the necessary finance to cover both the dowry and the wedding, permission was granted for the ceremony to go ahead. During the weeks that followed, Stanley presented the requested three goats to Naomi's parents in exchange for his bride. The balance of the dowry would be paid in cash just before the wedding. After the ceremony, many more gifts would be brought to her family to show the groom's appreciation of the good wife he had obtained.

It was going to be a church wedding for a modern young couple used to city life, so they went window shopping together in Nairobi, deciding how they wanted this important day to be celebrated. Later they did their individual shopping, accompanied by the chief bridesmaid and the best man respectively. Preparations were complicated, given the distance of their home places from Nairobi.

All their Nairobi friends were invited to the wedding, which would take place at Stanley's home place in Kangundo, 120 kilometres away from Naomi's family. Apart from the all-important wedding dress for the bride and wedding suit for the groom, the shopping list included clothes for both sets of parents and for anyone else in the family who could not afford to buy for themselves. The tall, iced wedding cake, centrepiece of the food table, would be supplemented by rice, chapattis, sodas, *mokimo* – a traditional food made with potatoes – and other special meat dishes created for the occasion. The decorations were very important – balloons, ribbons, and banners bearing their English names: "Naomi weds Stanley".

On 11 May 2000, the wedding took place in Kangundo, in a church on the outskirts of town. A dignified service conducted by the bishop was followed by a noisy reception in the church compound. The ceremonial cutting of the cake caused great excitement, with everyone impatient to taste this unusual food; some had never seen anything like it before. After a full day of celebrations, the young couple left the crowd of well-wishers behind, to spend two weeks alone together on their honeymoon near Lake Nakuru in Central Kenya.

Back in Nairobi, having moved into Stanley's small

two-roomed house, Naomi continued to work as a secretary, coming home to cook for her new husband in the evening. She loved the buzz of city life, revelling in all the excitement and opportunities it offered. When the young couple learned they were expecting their first baby, they moved with great anticipation to a larger house, in order to accommodate their growing family.

One year after the wedding, their son was born.

The birth was difficult, with Naomi being rushed off to theatre for an emergency Caesarean section. For a while her life hung in the balance but as she regained consciousness she heard the magical words, "You have a lovely big baby boy."

Her response was immediate. "He will be Christ's. It is the love of God that has brought me through the surgery and kept the child safe." Together the relieved parents praised God for what he had done.

Naomi reflects, "We felt God had shown us such love, with me going to theatre, coming back to life, and the boy being born so healthy and well. We called him Chris Mwenda because it means 'the love of God'. I had so many complications during the pregnancy that we told each other that if this baby survived, it would be Christ's. We always felt his name was special."

Gradually she recovered, and a grateful Stanley brought his wife and son safely back home. Chris did well, giving them little trouble and much joy. The following year, they decided to build their own home in Kangundo, obliging Naomi to leave Nairobi to supervise the construction of the new house. Each weekend Stanley came from Nairobi and they went to church together on Sunday before he returned to the city in the company car.

Early on the morning of Sunday 21 September 2003, Stanley called Naomi from Nakuru where, contrary to his usual pattern, he had been working on the Saturday.

"I'm on my way home now. I'll be there in time for us to go to church together."

Asking the girl who helped her in the house to look after Chris, Naomi proceeded to prepare breakfast and get ready for church. Suddenly, she heard shouting and screaming outside: "The baby is in the water!" Immediately Naomi's thoughts flew to the nearby pit latrine in the process of construction by a neighbour; four and a half metres deep, it was covered with branches to deter anyone from walking over it. She knew as she dashed out of the house that the toddler had somehow managed to wander onto the thorny branches and fallen through into the water beneath.

Racing to the scene, wild thoughts flashing through her mind, she automatically called out to God.

"God, my baby is in the pit. He will die; that pit is too deep. My baby is down there and his daddy is on the way home. What will I do? Where do I go now?"

Ahead of her, a young man ran to the pit and quickly tied ropes round his body. Getting the crowd that had gathered around to hold the end of the ropes, he managed to walk crab-wise down the inside of the pit, grab the child, and bring him back up to ground level. Shocked and half-drowned, Chris was rushed to the health centre, where, to everyone's amazement, apart from being very frightened he seemed little the worse for his ordeal.

Naomi, however, took longer to recover. Traumatized by the morning's events, she was in a state of shock, thinking of what might have been. She was aware of little groups of people talking quietly together near the health centre; perhaps they were discussing Chris's accident. Although she wondered briefly what was consuming their interest, she was too busy trying to reach Stanley on his mobile to think about anything else. He must be nearly home by now and she was unsure how to break the news of Chris's narrow brush with death. It was unusual to have difficulty getting through on his phone.

Returning home, she found no sign of Stanley; the house was quiet and empty. Preoccupied with Chris's condition, it was only as the day wore on that she became aware of people in the area around the house talking to each other; some story was still circulating but she was not part of it. Wondering what was going on, she kept waiting for Stanley to appear, but there was no sign of him, nor any answer from his phone. When a solemn-faced group of men entered her house at 9.00 that evening and stood around looking awkward, fear barrelled through her like a train in an endless tunnel.

"Where is the father of Chris?" she asked in a voice tight with dread. "I know something is happening; I can't get him on the phone; I haven't been to the shopping centre to hear the news. Please just tell me."

Slowly one of the men came up to her. "I'm sorry, Naomi. He had an accident this morning; he has just passed on."

"Passed on? What do you mean?" Naomi was bewildered.

"He had an accident just after phoning you this morning. Some children were crossing the road to go to church and he swerved to avoid them and rolled the car on the rough road. There were two other passengers in the car and he told them he was rushing home to go to church with you. They are fine, but Stanley died on the spot. He was only a short distance from here when it happened. We were afraid to tell you, thinking it would be too much of a shock for you after the fright you had this morning with Chris. People said this second happening would crush you, but you have to know now."

Naomi's face is grave as she tries to explain to me how she felt. "I just saw blackness; I couldn't see any light. I didn't have anything to say. I just knew my life had changed. As I was crying, I was thinking, 'I have been living with this lovely man for such a short time. How can I live without him now? How will I make it? I don't have any job. I already left my job to look after the baby.'" Her thoughts roamed from inexpressible grief to the practical problems now confronting her.

Even before the first storm of grief had passed she was conscious of an inner voice speaking to her spirit: "We know that in all things – *all* things – God works for the good of those who love him." She began to listen to other Scriptures that started flowing into her mind as God blessed her with his word. Bowing in submission to God's will she prayed, "God, I thank you for everything. You planned our life together, you gave us a baby, and now you have taken my husband. You know what is best for us."

The funeral was planned for the following Saturday. On the Monday after Stanley's death and throughout the week before the burial, Naomi was buoyed up by the words that God kept pouring into her mind. Somehow the power of God seemed to take over, in a way that was beyond her understanding, keeping her calm, giving her words of encouragement for the people who were gathering from all parts of the country, people who had known the family and wanted to identify with her in her grief. Her husband had been young, energetic, supportive to the community, and helpful to everyone in the home place. No one could believe he was gone. Faced with his young widow, who seemed to have gained access to some power beyond herself, people were taken aback.

"Naomi, are you preaching to us? We are supposed to be ministering to *you*."

Quietly she accepted that God was with her in such a way that she was able to greet those who were grieving, bringing them a message of comfort from his word. She was aware that it was not of herself, but, in a way that no one could understand, God had taken over the situation for his glory.

She felt upheld by God throughout that week, receiving strength for herself and others as they prepared for the funeral. Finally, the day came.

Naomi recalls her feelings. "On Saturday we had the burial. We laid him peacefully to rest. We grieved, but God comforted us. We knew he was with us in this hard time as he had been with us in the good times."

Once the funeral was over, Naomi realized she had to start life again with her son. It would be a different life, standing alone, thinking about where to find the finance needed to move forward. Isolated at home, she threw all her questions towards God. "We have to make a new start now. How do I help the boy? How do I get finances? How do I get work so my son gets all he needs?" They were daunting questions, to which she had no answer. She waited for God's word, however. She knew he would not abandon her.

Unexpectedly, Stanley's company contacted her, informing her that as a widow she was entitled to compensation. It was not a huge amount, but, as she prayed for wisdom, Naomi realized that if she used the money to get a college education, she could find pensionable work which would give her and her son security for the future.

With this in mind, she did a two-year teacher training course in a college about 200 kilometres away, leaving Chris in the care of her mother during term time and looking forward to being with him during the holidays. Some of Stanley's money paid for her fees, and some went to her mother to care for Chris. She concentrated as much effort as possible on her studies, but from time to time she would get a phone call that caused her to rush back to her unoccupied house in Kangundo, where her in-laws were attempting to appropriate her belongings.

Despite these setbacks, she did well on her course and everyone celebrated with her when she graduated in 2006. Naomi, delighted to be reunited with her son, immediately began to look for work.

Assured that she was guaranteed employment in a

government school because of her high grades, Naomi and Chris moved to Nairobi where there were more opportunities. While waiting for a government job, she took temporary work in an independent school where the pay and conditions were very poor. Forced to live in a corrugated iron house in a slum area of the city, she slept on the floor with her son. The job was difficult, the money it brought in was barely enough to live on, and her surroundings were grim. Every morning Naomi prayed, "God, help me to find another job away from here. I don't want to bring up my child in this place. Open a better way."

One Sunday she went along as usual to her local church service. A huge crowd had gathered to hear a speaker from Australia. In the course of his address, he spoke words that seemed to resonate in her heart: "God is going to lift people from this church and send them to far-off places they have never been before, to do his work."

Struck by these words, Naomi went outside to think about what it might mean. Trying to understand what God was saying, she began to talk to him about it.

"There are many people here in this church who are very capable. Send the people with money and cars to do your work."

But the answer came almost immediately: "I use the weak vessel to shame the strong."

Struggling to grasp this thought, she could not get the words out of her mind in the following days. On the Wednesday of that week she received a phone call from one of her former college tutors.

"Hi, Naomi. Where are you now? Have you got a job? I know someone who is looking for teachers in a place called Bombi in Galana."

Naomi had never heard of it. "Where is this place? Is it far from Nairobi?"

"It's on the coast, nearly 600 kilometres away. The nearest town is Malindi. An Irish missionary working there came to Malindi Education Office looking for a Christian teacher for the school. I said, 'I know the right person. I taught her in college. I know her faith in God. Let me contact her.' What do you think? Would you be willing to come to Galana? It is very remote and very different from Nairobi."

Naomi was excited. Was this the far-off place that God had spoken to her about on Sunday?

"I would like to think about it. I am in Nairobi but maybe I can get there. How do you get to Malindi from here?"

The more she thought about it, the more obvious it seemed that this was God's plan. Unable to afford the fare for such a journey, she found that everything was organized for her, and almost before she knew it she found herself in Malindi, certificates in hand, being interviewed for the job.

She was unsurprised to be told she had been successful in obtaining the post. It seemed that God was going before her. When she was informed that the starting salary would be three times what she was earning in Nairobi, it seemed like a miracle. She struggled to keep her composure.

"I was crying in my heart and saying, 'This must be God.' I was giving him thanks and saying, 'You are so wonderful.' I could not take in what he was doing for us."

After the euphoria of Malindi came the rough journey to Galana. Reality began to set in as she realized the remoteness and isolation of the area, with no access to all the facilities on her doorstep in Nairobi. Finally they reached the newly built school and staff accommodation. Naomi realized that she had moved from living in a noisy, frightening slum to her own peaceful, two-roomed brick house, with other teachers and project workers living around her. Her heart opened in praise to God for all that he was doing.

The school had just opened the year before and the new teachers quickly developed a bond as they put all their efforts into building up this facility for a community desperate for help. Chris, however, was unimpressed with his new home.

"Mum, you have brought me to this place where there is no milk and no bread. Why did we leave Nairobi?" Naomi's reasons made little sense to a six-year-old.

In a way that she was unable fully to explain to Chris, Naomi felt a sense of call to the people of this challenging region. "Although my surroundings in Nairobi were difficult, it was more convenient to live there. Here in Galana the conditions were better for me in some ways, but in others it was a hard place because of the remoteness of the area. I knew, however, that God had brought me here for a reason and was preparing me for a wider ministry."

She began to receive invitations to go elsewhere in the country to speak about the work in Bombi School. The words that God had spoken to her through the Australian speaker in Nairobi constantly echoed in her mind: "This is the place. I have sent you here for my purposes."

In 2007, a team from Carnmoney in Northern Ireland came to the area for a few weeks, organizing a variety of activities both physical and spiritual for the young people from the school. Derek asked Naomi if she would be available to work with the team, helping them to fit into life in Bombi. As part of their work, they brought wonderful new materials for use in the Sunday school. The children loved the exciting illustrations of Bible stories and Naomi found she enjoyed teaching the younger ones so much that she never wanted to miss it. She continued to use the resources after the team's departure.

Touched by the little ones often walking a long distance and arriving hungry at church, Naomi started to provide porridge for the children. As the numbers grew, she was thrilled by their hunger, not just for physical food but for the word of God.

"Sometimes I used my computer to show them Christian movies and they really enjoyed it. The church was growing and we were delighted that so many young people wanted to come and hear what God was saying to them."

Naomi's experience with the team from Ireland awoke in her a realization of the work that was needed over the whole Galana area, with so many knowing little about God. She was conscious of a twofold calling – to her paid employment and also to the ministry that God had for her in that place.

"It was difficult because I was not born here and the lifestyle is different. At first Galana seemed like a wilderness, where the climate and conditions were harsh for those not used to them. The school was 150 kilometres from Malindi, the nearest town, so obtaining even basic items was a problem. To use public transport meant walking seven kilometres and crossing the river. Sometimes I would stop and say, 'God, is it really you who sent me here?' But always the answer came back: 'It is I. All things are possible.'"

Before she knew it, a great love grew in Naomi's heart for the people around her. She explains how she first realized what was happening.

"When the school closed for the holidays and I went up country to my home place, I felt as if I was leaving very small kids, with no one to care for them. I knew I had no choice but to come back and carry on the work here."

Naomi knew she needed to lean on the grace of God to live and work in Galana. When she had first heard the Australian's sermon in Nairobi, she had found it hard to imagine that she was one of the people God was sending out. Yet she remembered how both Moses and Jeremiah had protested their inadequacy when God called them; God sent them despite their insecurities, and equipped them for the task.

"God did not let me down. I had to lift those people of Bombi before the Lord until God worked in their hearts. We arranged special times of outreach to go to the homes of the people to speak to them about Christ and the word of God. Sometimes it was difficult because of their culture and lifestyle. They did not want to change their way of life and believe in God. There was a big problem with alcohol abuse, for example. But we did not give up. We encouraged them to read the word of God and we tried to show them how their life could change."

Three years on, the school is showing encouraging signs of growth. At first there were many more boys than girls, as families married off their daughters while they were still young, sometimes in their early teens, rather than allowing them to attend school. Gradually, however, the value of education, even for the girls, is beginning to be understood and more girls are now in school. A major step forward came when a partnership developed with a school in Ireland, with exchange visits of teachers between the two schools. Some of the Irish teachers started a club in Bombi School, where girls could learn practical skills such as jewellery-making, or using a sewing machine. As the girls became excited about developing talents they could use for the rest of their lives, education as a whole became more attractive to them.

Naomi reflects, "The school is doing well and we are happy for the girls who now have a passion to study and be in school instead of being married. It is great to see all the development that has taken place in the area."

As friendships developed with the group from Ireland, the way suddenly opened for Naomi to fulfil a long-deferred dream. Her new-found Irish friends managed to obtain sponsorship for her to do a degree in education at Nairobi University.

"It was a miracle. God opened the way for me to get to university, even though my parents were not able to send me. I teach in Bombi School during term time, and then attend university in Nairobi during the school holidays.

I hope to graduate at the end of next year. It is a lot of work to teach in school during the week and Sunday school at the weekend, keep up with my university studies, *and* prepare for university examinations, but I am so grateful for the opportunity, and God gives me the strength to do everything I need to do."

As Chris grew, he began to voice questions about his situation. One day he said to Naomi, "I see other children with a dad. Now where is mine?"

Naomi talked to him about his father's death. The next time they were back in Kangundo, they went together to the grave.

"This is where your dad was laid," she said gently. "He loved you, but he died in that car crash and he is in heaven now. One day we will see him again. I know you really miss having a dad, but we have to trust God. He will supply all we need."

Chris is now at boarding school, where he has access to the resources he needs for his education. As he is an intelligent boy with a bright, questioning mind, Naomi is delighted to see him doing so well in school.

For herself, she continues to put her trust in God.

"There are lots of challenges. Sometimes it is hard because I have to do all the planning and working things out myself, but I just ask for God's assistance not to make the wrong choice. I know that God is with me and that verse is still true that he gave me all those years ago: 'All things work together for good'."

This community, with few commodities available locally, offers us generous refreshments before our return to Malindi. A group of well-wishers escorts us to our vehicle and sees us off with many calls of goodwill for the homeward journey and cheerful waves of farewell. Leaving Galana, passing small villages of mud houses and young children herding animals, we drive at a steady speed over bumps and gullies, rocky stretches and sandy surfaces. In places the road falls away steeply into a daunting ditch on either side, leaving a high single lane in the middle. When we meet an oncoming car it is a matter of bravado which vehicle manages to hold the centre ground. A large hole in the road catches us unawares and the vehicle plunges into a dip; we bounce hard, straining against the seat belts, and the banter from the back seat escalates.

Dusty and shaken, we return to Malindi, past the market where the stallholders are packing up their goods, back to our apartment where a refreshing breeze blows through open windows and the mosquito net is draped reassuringly round the bed. Clean water, a cup of tea, a shower, food – luxuries we take for granted every day.

The next day we pack up and prepare for our return flight to Belfast. Eddie and Mary look somewhat forlorn as we say our goodbyes. Much as they feel called to the work in Galana, they will miss Ireland and the link with their home country that our presence somehow brings. Various teams are booked to come and help with work on the bridge in the near future, which will be an encouragement and support as they go forward.

As we board the plane for home, we take a last look at the red earth and bright light of Kenya. We leave Africa inspired by all we have seen and challenged by the faith of those we leave behind.

Epilogue

Twenty-four hours later, with the smooth co-operation of modern transport, we are back in Ireland. For the first few days we are struck by the contrasts between Africa and Ireland. We regard the cool grey skies of the Irish summer and long for the heat and light of the African sun. The material comforts of our home and lifestyle make us uneasy as we remember situations of desperate need. Small inconveniences fade into insignificance in the face of the tragedies we have witnessed.

As the days pass, the contrasts diminish and we settle back into the usual busyness of life. What remains, however, is the deep impact made by those we have met, the resilience, faith, joy, and care for others that unite African and European as they trust God for the future and work together to bring God's love to those around them.

As I go to bed at night, unhampered by mosquito net or unusual noises, I see again the faces of Africa – solemn faces of young children in a hospital ward, tragic faces of young people who have suffered at the hands of others, bright faces of young men fizzing with enthusiasm for what they can achieve with God's help, caring faces of young women concerned to reach out to others, worn faces of those further down the road, looking back over a journey of challenges but seeing how they have proved God in all the turns of the path.

The images drift and mingle until I see another face and hear a voice:

> *Therefore go and make disciples of all nations, baptizing them in the name of the Father and of the Son and of the Holy Spirit, and teaching them to obey everything I have commanded you. And surely I am with you always, to the very end of the age (Matthew 28:19–20).*

> *For I was hungry and you gave me something to eat, I was thirsty and you gave me something to drink, I was a stranger and you invited me in, I needed clothes and you clothed me, I was sick and you looked after me, I was in prison and you came to visit me (Matthew 25:35–36).*

> *Truly I tell you, whatever you did for one of the least of these brothers and sisters of mine, you did for me (Matthew 25:40).*

Author's note

If you have been touched by anything you have read in this book and would like to explore how you could help in these or similar situations, please contact the author through her website: www.jeangibson.co.uk

Notes

Chapter 1: Joy

1. http://wikitravel.org/en/Tanzania
2. *Nsima* is a staple food made from local maize meal.

Chapter 2: Marcus

1. A *chitenge* is a length of colourful printed cotton fabric worn wrapped round the body.
2. David Smith, *The Guardian*, 24 August 2009: http://www.guardian.co.uk/world/2009/aug/24/malawi-child-tobacco-pickers-poisoned

Chapter 3: Mphatso

1. http://www.who.int/gho/hiv/en/
2. http://www.avert.org/aids-malawi.htm

Chapter 4: Maria

1. http://www.who.int/tb/hiv/faq/en/

Chapter 8: Kasoni

1. A *manyatta* is a traditional Samburu settlement of houses enclosed by a thorn fence.
2. http://allafrica.com/stories/201104140205.html
3. *Eliminating Female Genital Mutilation – An interagency statement*, World Health Organization, 2008, http://www.unifem.org/attachments/products/fgm_statement_2008_eng.pdf

Chapter 9: Nabiki

1. http://www.guardian.co.uk/society/2011/jun/26/10-million-child-brides-each-year-charity-warns

Chapter 10: Guyo

1. A *kanga* is a piece of colourful printed cotton fabric worn wrapped around the body.
2. A *matatu* is a local minibus taxi.